PENGUIN BUSINESS
UNLOCKING UNICORN SECRETS

Kushal Lodha is the founder of KAGR, an ed-tech platform in finance upskilling. He is a qualified CA (with all-India ranks across all levels). He is a part-time creator with over five lakh-plus followers on social media cumulatively. He was awarded the LinkedIn's Top Voice for 2022.

He is the author of *Acing CA*, a #1 Amazon bestseller, which talks about his CA journey and opportunities for CAs in and outside India.

Ishan Sharma is the co-founder of MarkitUp, a content agency, and is a content creator with over 1.5 million followers across social media. He has delivered speeches at colleges like IIT Jodhpur.

Ishan is also the author of *Crush It on LinkedIn: Build Your Brand, Get Hired & Expand Your Business*, a book where he shares how to get opportunities using LinkedIn. He has taught Python programming and full stack development on Unacademy, having coached more than 1000 students for over 350 hrs.

T0017880

Celebrating 35 Years of
Penguin Random House India

ADVANCE PRAISE FOR THE BOOK

'In *Unlocking Unicorn Secrets*, Kushal and Ishan bring you the remarkable success stories of India's unicorn founders. This book serves as a powerful reminder that successful entrepreneurs are those who address user pain points, embrace resilience in the face of adversity and cultivate teams with complementary skills. Discover the secrets to unlocking your entrepreneurial potential within these pages' —Arundhati Bhattacharya, former chairperson, State Bank of India

'Inspiration awaits within the pages of *Unlocking Unicorn Secrets*. Kushal and Ishan have thoughtfully curated the stories of India's most prominent unicorn founders, offering readers a glimpse into their extraordinary achievements. This book is a must-read for aspiring entrepreneurs, as it unveils the secrets that can turn dreams into reality'—Harsh Mariwala, chairman, Marico

'There are a lot of challenges that entrepreneurs have to face, especially during their initial days. This book will help you understand how to tackle these challenges and stay ahead of the curve. Best wishes to Kushal and Ishan for coming up with such a great book'—Nirmal Jain, chairman, India Infoline Group

'Growing a start-up into a stable business is challenging irrespective of the founder's background or the capital/resources available. While this is common knowledge, some of the stories of start-ups and founders going through difficult times need to be told. And this book captures some of those untold stories of building teams, being open to feedback and finding the right mentors, all of which can help budding entrepreneurs with their start-ups. Wishing Kushal and Ishan the very best and am sure this book will help lots of young entrepreneurs out there'—Nikhil Kamath, co-founder, Zerodha

'Kushal and Ishan have written an insightful book that delves into the formation of India's most successful unicorns. Their narrative is based on first-hand interviews with founders who have shared real and personal stories of their struggles and successes in building billion-dollar organizations. Over my own entrepreneurial journey, I have constantly benefited from reading numerous biographies and accounts of iconic entrepreneurs. I hope the stories contained in this book will continue to inspire the emerging generation and provide a deeper understanding of the rich Indian start-up landscape'—Bhavin Turakhia, founder, Zeta

'Kushal and Ishan, two ambitious young individuals, embarked on an extraordinary mission to uncover the secrets of success. Through a series of captivating interviews, they connected with the founders of billion-dollar businesses, delving into their inspiring stories of perseverance, sacrifice and triumph. With each encounter, Kushal and Ishan gained invaluable insights into the minds of these remarkable entrepreneurs, revealing universal principles that underpin success. Join them on a riveting journey that will empower and inspire you to unleash your own potential and achieve greatness'—Alakh Pandey, founder, PhysicsWallah

'India added twenty-two unicorns in 2022. But that's just an imaginary creature. What is real are the struggles, the commitment, the tenacity and ambition of the founders and their teams. The story that is rarely heard, beyond just the billion-dollar valuation. I am glad Ishan and Kushal chose to share their stories. To inspire an entire generation of entrepreneurs in this country. More power to those who dream big and dream crazy'—Ankur Warikoo, content creator with eight million-plus followers

'Becoming an entrepreneur is not an easy task. It requires courage, consistency and ability to handle failures. This book talks about the zero to one stories of founders who have made it big. I will recommend this to all the aspiring founders who are looking for some inspiration' —Raj Shamani, founder, House of X, and content creator with three million-plus followers

UNLOCKING UNICORN SECRETS

BEHIND THE SCENES OF INDIA'S BILLION-DOLLAR START-UPS

Kushal Lodha & Ishan Sharma

PENGUIN
BUSINESS

An imprint of Penguin Random House

PENGUIN BUSINESS

USA | Canada | UK | Ireland | Australia
New Zealand | India | South Africa | China | Singapore

Penguin Business is part of the Penguin Random House group of companies
whose addresses can be found at global.penguinrandomhouse.com

Published by Penguin Random House India Pvt. Ltd
4th Floor, Capital Tower 1, MG Road,
Gurugram 122 002, Haryana, India

First published in Penguin Business by Penguin Random House India 2023

ISBN 9780143461609

Typeset in RequiemText by MAP Systems, Bengaluru, India

www.penguin.co.in

To the youth of India,
who fearlessly pursue their wildest dreams

Contents

Foreword

I am delighted to learn about the book titled *Unlocking Unicorn Secrets* written by Kushal Lodha and Ishan Sharma, which highlights the remarkable success stories of India's twenty unicorn founders and their achievements.

Start-ups are the backbone of 'New India'. Initiatives such as Startup India and Digital India, launched by Honorable Prime Minister Shri Narendra Modi, are envisioned to catalyse India's start-up culture and make India the largest start-up nation globally. Today, the Indian start-up ecosystem is the third largest ecosystem in the world and has experienced unprecedented growth in the number of unicorns. Our young and talented workforce, coupled with a rapidly expanding digital infrastructure, has provided a fertile ground for Indian start-ups to flourish. It is noteworthy that during India's ongoing G20 presidency, the Startup20 Engagement Group has been initiated for the first time which would go a long way in promoting the growth of start-ups not only in India but across the world.

This book explores the stories of India's twenty successful and brightest unicorn start-ups through a series of interviews with their founders and will help in imbibing the entrepreneurial mindset in our nation's youth. The book also highlights the untold stories behind building these successful start-ups including team building, fundraising, scaling their businesses and overcoming challenges, among others. It will assist, motivate and inspire young minds to build and leverage their start-ups to new heights and foster a deeper understanding of the diverse Indian start-up ecosystem.

I am hopeful that the readers, especially the younger generation, will be benefited from the immense hard work that has been put into writing the book. Together, let us continue to unlock unicorn secrets and build a brighter future for India and the world. I congratulate the authors for bringing out this remarkable composition and wish them all success for their future endeavours.

8 July 2023   Piyush Goyal
                         Minister of Commerce and Industry;
                         Consumer Affairs, Food and Public
                              Distribution; and Textiles,
                                  Government of India

Introduction

Two kids with big dreams—that's what we have always been; whether it was Kushal bagging multiple degrees and working in an excellent company in his early twenties, or Ishan having his full-fledged agency at twenty and dropping out of BITS Pilani! Since we also wanted to make it big in our lives, we always wondered what it took to get there. So, we thought, why not ask the people who have actually got there and created billion-dollar businesses? And that's what we did.

We started reaching out to people, hundreds of them. We didn't know what the right way of approaching them was, so we obtained a list of the unicorn start-ups in the country, found out the email-ids of their founders and started sending emails to them with insane subject lines.

No, trust us, the subject lines were really insane. One of them was, 'Read Now or Regret Later', ha ha! We did receive some responses, but we could not reach out to most of whom we had mailed. But that made us realize that we needed to change our methods.

From the first mail to each start-up founder to the interview, it took us two to three months. We had to shift to a more sensible way, and that was to approach the public relations (PR) teams of these companies instead. It also turned out to be the right way of going about it.

Don't get us wrong, but the right way doesn't mean the easy way. We had to email hundreds of people and follow up with them several times. We were rejected many times, but this did not dishearten us. Most of the people would leave us on read and some directly said no. That was still better than having interviews scheduled and then getting ghosted, though. We had to get on multiple calls with PR teams to explain to them how we were authentic people and what the motive behind our wanting to write this book was. Again, don't get us wrong, we are not complaining; we just want to tell you that doing something is hard and it is your tenacity that will bring you success. It did for us, didn't it?

We made several mistakes down the line, like underestimating Bengaluru traffic and the Delhi heat, entering the wrong address on Google Maps and almost missing some of our meetings, being late to some of them and missing out on an opportunity or two as a result of it. But the experience we have gained from the entire process of writing this book will stand us in good stead as we set the stage for what we do next.

The first time we travelled to record an interview was to OfBusiness and Oxyzo, and what an experience it was! When we reached their office, we were greeted by the co-founder, Ruchi Kalra herself, and we realized these companies do not employ assistants and the executives do everything on their own. When we went inside the office, we saw that there were no cabins, not even for the C-suite executives and founders, and that speaks volumes about the culture of a company.

Most of the founders we met appreciated our hands-on approach. During the initial interviews, we were doing everything on our own—from arranging meetings to setting up cameras to conducting interviews—and that really impressed the founders. They saw two young guys working hard for something they wanted, and, looking at the zeal in their eyes, agreed to be interviewed.

The founders we interviewed also helped us connect with other founders. The first founder referred us to three more founders, the next few referred us to more, and so on. When we interviewed them, we asked them about their childhood, the stories of their start-ups from the time they were just an idea to the time they fetched their first set of customers, what skills they looked for while hiring people, the sacrifices they had to make, how they dealt with fear of failure, etc. But, most importantly, we threw a curveball at them at the end of the interview: 'What would you have wanted to ask yourselves, had you been in our shoes?' Almost all of the founders we spoke to thought for a minute or two before answering that. We got some really good answers to this question, and we can't wait for you to read them too.

For many other questions, a lot of the founders, surprisingly, had similar answers, which makes us wonder if there is actually a secret sauce behind building a successful start-up.

Let's get started and learn the unicorn secrets from the unicorn founders themselves.

I

CarDekho Group

Start-up Name	CarDekho Group
Headquarters	Jaipur, Rajasthan, India
Sector	Automotive, E-commerce
Founders	Amit Jain and Anurag Jain
Founded	2008
Valuation	$1.2 billion (October 2021)
Website	cardekho.com

About CarDekho Group

CarDekho Group is India's leading auto tech-solutions provider. Established in 2008 by brothers Amit Jain and Anurag Jain, who are IIT graduates, CarDekho Group started off as an online portal for car reviews in the tier-II city of Rajasthan, Jaipur. Since its inception, the brainchild of the Jain brothers has grown tremendously from being a car review platform to a conglomerate having a house of brands in operations and a unicorn in valuation. It also has various platforms under its umbrella, such as BikeDekho, CarDekho group, ZigWheels and PowerDrift, through which it hosts more than 62 million monthly active users.

At a time when most start-ups think they have to move to Bengaluru, Gurugram or Pune in order to scale, Amit (the new Shark on Shark Tank India) and Anurag built CarDekho Group ground up in a tier-two city, Jaipur. Not just that, they even turned it into a unicorn.

'From middle class to unicorn.'

CarDekho Group was founded by two brothers, Amit and Anurag Jain, in 2008. The Jains come from a middle-class family, and, just like children in most middle-class families, they too were asked to focus on academics.

Amit wasn't an academically good kid. After passing out of twelfth standard, he sat for the IIT entrance exam, which he did not get through, having scored zero in one of the subjects. At that time, his father used to live in Mumbai for work, so he decided to go stay with him. His father personally tutored him, and Amit worked tirelessly for months to prepare for his entrance exams. He took the test again and went from zero in one of the subjects to a full score. And that's how he got admission to IIT Delhi.

How did an average kid go from flunking an exam to joining IIT Delhi? He did it solely because of his hard work. Amit says he is not a very brilliant guy, but he is definitely a very hardworking one.

Having been brought up in a middle-class family, the values of respect, ambition, hard work and integrity were instilled in the duo from very early on. These values have helped them stay on their chosen paths and come out of the mistakes and failures they faced in their career to become two of India's biggest entrepreneurs.

'Can we impact India?'

The co-founders found themselves pondering over this question while starting CarDekho Group in a garage. They didn't have a concrete answer back then, but they knew that they would give the venture their all. They saw an opportunity to make a real difference in the lives of Indian consumers by providing them with access to comprehensive and reliable information about cars, and they took it.

This early question as to whether they could impact India or not has been answered many times over now. CarDekho Group has not only impacted the Indian automobile market but has also had a far-reaching impact on the lives of Indian consumers.

'How big can you dream?'

Like Amit, Anurag too went to IIT Delhi. The brothers recall how their exposure at the institute to new people and ideas helped shape their own ideas. When you are around ambitious minds with extravagant dreams of doing something big, you tend to wonder how large a dream you can possibly nurse too. And that was what changed inside them at IIT.

Amit travelled a lot in his college days. He went on many road trips to the hills of Nainital and Mussoorie. He credits these trips with shaping him into who he is today. When you come from a tier-2 city and start travelling, you realize how impactful it is. These trips boosted his confidence and helped him become street-smart. He finds it very important to step out of your comfort zone and explore the world because you never know what kind of impact it may have on your life.

While Amit was already in IIT, Anurag was still struggling to get into one. He dropped a year, went to Delhi for preparation and gave the exam. Unfortunately, for the first time in IIT's history, the paper was leaked, and he had to retake the exam. Despite this setback, he managed to clear the exam and finally secured his place at IIT Delhi.

Amit and Anurag both got jobs through campus placements. Amit was employed at Dallas in a US-based company. Having grown up in a joint family in India, he found people in the US quite individualistic. For instance, he made a random visit to an NRI friend from his office to hang out with and was greeted with a very dry 'Did I call you?' response from him. He started missing his home and the welcoming nature of Indian people. He didn't like being too far away from home, so after about a year in the US, he came back to India and joined the same company's Bengaluru office.

'Life happens sometimes. You can't run from it.'

Amit and Anurag faced a difficult time when their father was diagnosed with cancer. Despite various treatments, he unfortunately passed away after fourteen months. When the doctors informed them that his condition was beyond treatment, their father expressed his desire to spend his remaining days in Kashmir, where he had honeymooned and cherished happy memories. He wanted to be surrounded by beauty and positivity during his final days.

This was very inspirational for the brothers, that their father wanted to be happy even during the saddest of his days. But this loss marked a pivotal moment in their lives, forever altering the course of their journeys.

They let go of their jobs and came back home with a heavy heart and just one belief—that they would make something work, no matter how hard it was.

'Hume laga hum IIT se hain, fod denge!'
[We thought since we have graduated from an IIT, we'll do amazing business!]

After moving to Jaipur, Amit and Anurag decided to take over their father's gemstone business. As proud IIT graduates, they were confident in their abilities and believed their education would allow them to excel in the business world. However, they soon discovered that running a business was harder than they had anticipated. The gemstone trade was different from the corporate world, and they struggled to adapt.

It was difficult to manage the finances and resources of the business, and they realized that frugality was an important factor. From staying in five-star hotels and flying business class, suddenly they were looking for budget hotels and flying economy class. 'Despite our best efforts, we soon realized that an IIT education does not prepare you for the practicalities of running a business,' says Amit.

Eventually, being engineers by qualification, they decided to build something they were both good at, and GirnarSoft was born. It was a company that provided digital solutions and consulting to other businesses.

'If you do good, it comes back in different forms.'

Anurag reached out to one of his ex-colleagues from his previous IT company who was just establishing a start-up in the US. That was the first company that GirnarSoft on-boarded as a client.

The second project came from Amit's ex-employer, Trilogy. This was all due to the amazing skills and conviction the Jains had displayed during their corporate tenures. They were able to build the trust factor with colleagues, which is very important for the kick-starting of any form of business. Anurag also says it was great to have on-boarded two new clients in the first month itself, as their burn rate became zero.

'I have seen very ordinary people become extraordinary in life.'

The Jains were based out of Jaipur, so they decided to hire and promote local talent. They soon realized how hungry tier-2 and tier-3 city people are for opportunities to learn, grow and prove themselves. He on-boarded them and trained them. Today, these same young people who joined them as interns hold CXO-level positions in the company.

When young men and women from tier-2 or tier-3 cities take on a job, they have a fire within to prove themselves. Amit believes that all you need to do is fan the flames of this fire.

Amit's aim from the very beginning was to build a unicorn—a billion-dollar company. While he and Anurag had built an amazing team with talented and determined people, GirnarSoft wasn't growing as fast as they wanted it to. They also didn't see fast growth happening any time soon for a company such as theirs, as there were already many established players in the market. They knew they had to start a product-based business. So, they spent the next few years just experimenting with different ventures.

'You learn every day, you fail every day, you change the code every day.'

Working in a fast-growing start-up allows for a dynamic and constantly evolving work environment, where employees are encouraged to learn, fail and change the course every day. The fast-paced nature of start-ups provides ample opportunities for growth and personal development, as well as the chance to work on cutting-edge technologies and innovative ideas.

'Feet on the ground, eye on the sky.'

Amit describes CarDekho Group's workplace as an office with a bunch of very ambitious, hungry, humble people who function like a family. He says that he has always tried to create a fearless culture at CarDekho Group. While the brothers were trying to come up with a name for the start-up, they had initially decided on ECarsInfo. An intern, upon hearing the name, immediately said, 'That's a terrible name.' This led them to change the name to CarDekho Group.

One of the key advantages of working in a start-up is the constant feedback that is available, and this is a two-way street. Founders and employees both give feedback to each other. There is no traditional hierarchy, and the more open culture allows for ideas and feedback to flow freely to and from all levels of the organization. Employees contribute to the growth and success of the company, and their ideas and suggestions are not just heard but also acted upon.

'Experiences per year is more important than years of experience.'

It doesn't matter where you have worked and for how long; what matters is how much have you learned and how have you grown every year. People do not stay with a company for the money they get from it; they stay because they are eager to learn and grow at the company. Start-ups are very dynamic and people there get to learn something new almost every day.

Amit believes that passion is very important for a person to grow, be it in a start-up or a traditional business. People who are passionate about their work are more likely to be motivated, engaged and committed to achieving the company's goals. They also bring to the company a level of energy and enthusiasm that is contagious and inspires others to do their best work.

So, when hiring, you should look for people who have more experience per year than more years of experience.

'There should be a better way of doing it!'

While GirnarSoft was doing well and growing at a decent rate, Amit and Anurag were still searching for their billion-dollar idea. In 2008, they went to an Auto Expo at Pragati Maidan, Delhi; and it was while going through the car info brochures that the CarDekho Group idea struck.

They set up the website within the next six months and uploaded data on to it. They kept updating it, constantly adding new features to improve the consumer experience. It took them only two years to become India's largest automobile website in terms of traffic.

CarDekho Group received its first funding in 2013. Until then the venture did not have even a Facebook or Google Ad account. All the traffic that flew in was completely organic. Amit's SEO strategies were doing their magic.

'Content is king!'

By providing valuable information to their customers, they were able to establish themselves as a trusted source and attract a large following. This, in turn, helped them generate traffic organically and grow their audience without having to spend any money on marketing.

'We have been sitting on a gold mine!'

A US-based company called Auto Trader was planning to expand globally and invited the Jains for a meet-up.

When they met the CEO and saw what Auto Trader had accomplished in the US, the brothers realized that they had been sitting on a gold mine all this time.

The shift in focus to the automobile world was a bold move, but it paid off for them. The founders were quickly able to tap into the vast potential of the automobile industry, and CarDekho Group quickly became a leader in the space. The company's focus on innovation and technology allowed it to offer a range of cutting-edge services and products, from vehicle comparisons and reviews to financing and insurance services—everything that automobile customers wanted.

They also acquired many start-ups in 2014, including a relatively similar start-up called Gaadi.com. Its co-founder Umang Kumar also joined the CarDekho Group team, to work alongside Amit and Anurag. The three of them now collectively look after the company.

'The idea is to not let any competition exist,' says Amit. To this end, they have also acquired ZigWheels, a similar platform that provides automotive industry news, reviews and advice to consumers.

Amit believes that when a start-up has a stable and strong foundation, growth becomes an inevitable outcome. This is why CarDekho Group has grown at an amazing rate of 70 per cent every year on average for the last ten years straight.

'Raise money for scaling vs survival!'

Amit's advice to young entrepreneurs is to raise money for the purpose of scaling their business. Scaling is essential for a start-up to grow, reach out to more customers and achieve its goals. However, it is important to note that scaling must be done in a strategic and sustainable manner.

Raising money for survival, on the other hand, can often be a sign that a start-up is not on the right track. It may indicate that the business is not generating enough revenue or that it is not well positioned to grow. This can be a significant setback for a young start-up and can limit its potential for future success. Anurag says, 'It's okay to make losses, but they should be added to profitability.' Most start-ups incur losses in the initial years, but those losses should ultimately be compensated for by profitability in the long run.

When raising money, it is important to consider dilution or the amount of ownership you are willing to give up in your company. It is different for different businesses and depends on the market conditions and your own long-term goals.

Amit suggests that if there is an opportunity to capture a large market share by raising a large round, even if it leads to more dilution, it is worth it for the long-term success of the company. The key is to focus on the goal and make decisions that will benefit the company in the long run.

'Every founder needs to be a fighter!'

Amit believes that start-up founders should have a strong network of advisers and mentors who can provide guidance and support as the business grows. This network can help founders navigate the challenges of starting a business and provide valuable insights and advice on how to scale the business successfully.

'Be more execution-focused, especially in the early stages,' says Amit. Apart from this, you need to identify your field of expertise, your own superpower. It can be digital marketing, research, or anything else. You have to find that spark that will fire you, and things will start to happen.

Our curveball: If they were in our shoes, what question would they like to ask themselves?

Anurag's answer is a testament to his fun-loving nature. In a very Kapil Sharma-esque way, he said, '*Itna sab kuch kiya, pandrah saal company banayi, unicorn banaya—toh fir humse milke kaisa lag raha hai?* [We have done so much, built a company over fifteen years, turned it into a unicorn—so how do you feel about meeting us?]'

And the room erupted with laughter.

2

Cars24

Start-up Name	Cars24
Headquarters	Gurgaon, Haryana, India
Sector	Automotive
Founders	Vikram Chopra, Ruchit Agarwal and Mehul Agrawal
Founded	2015
Valuation	$3.3 billion (December 2021)
Website	www.cars24.com

About Cars24

CARS24 is a cutting-edge e-commerce platform for pre-owned autos, including cars and bikes, which strives to make buying and selling autos

a breeze. The platform offers a wide range of certified cars along with smooth and convenient home delivery facilities with the click of a button.
— StartupTalky

'The gap in a market is an opportunity in disguise.'

Vikram Chopra, co-founder and CEO of Cars24, started the company because he saw a gap in the used car market in India. He noticed that the process of selling a used car was often stressful and time consuming for individuals, and there were very few options for selling a used car quickly and easily.

Vikram wanted to create a platform that would make the selling of a used car more convenient and efficient for both buyers and sellers. He also wanted to create a transparent and trustworthy platform for the sale of used cars, giving buyers more confidence about their purchase.

Starting and building a company, especially a successful one, is a complex process, and it is hard to predict the outcome. Vikram had a vision for the company and believed in its potential for success, but the rapid growth and high valuation of Cars24 exceeded his initial expectations.

Vikram recalled his childhood days, growing up in a small town with little to no amenities. Back in the 1990s, there was no Internet, and he didn't even have a TV at home. As he grew up, he saw people around him buying things he could not afford; bikes, mobiles, computers, etc. He was left with a lingering desire to one day have all this, everything that he has missed out on. But his childhood experience of deprivation not only helped him learn to control his desires but also to enjoy whatever he did manage to acquire.

Vikram eventually landed a job as a business analyst at McKinsey.

'What I was doing at McKinsey was very counterintuitive to what people were advising me to do.'

Vikram's father was an engineer, and Vikram grew up seeing him work at factories. This was a huge reason he found himself attracted to projects that were very grounded. He was not too interested in projects in the fields of telecom, financial services, or infrastructure, which people usually look for while joining a company like McKinsey. Hence, his experience there was different from those of others there.

He then moved on to become an investment analyst at Sequoia Capital. Even at this point, he was not thinking of what would come up next, let alone worry about it. 'I was just finding pockets of enjoyment,' he said.

But it wasn't enough, and he wanted more. So, he left his job at Sequoia Capital and co-founded his first start-up called FabFurnish, an online store for furniture. Vikram says that while his team made a lot of mistakes in not planning sufficiently ahead and the venture eventually came to a halt, he enjoyed every second of it. His entrepreneurial journey had started, and he had finally found his home.

Having built and shut down an online e-commerce start-up, Vikram was finding that there were big shopping categories where people had had terrible experiences, especially in categories that did not work offline. He soon realized that furniture and cars both fell into that category.

They are both large products, equally difficult to put on display. Vikram and his team soon realized that selling and buying used cars is a process that should be moved solely to online platforms. That became their mission, and that is how Cars24 was born.

Ideas are not always going to strike people naturally. Sometimes you have to spend time looking for a problem, which will eventually land you an idea that can turn into an actual opportunity.

'Don't just focus on getting an idea! Focus on identifying a problem, you will automatically get an idea.'

Previously, whenever someone wanted to buy a used car, they would have to visit a minimum of five or six places just to come across some decent options. Besides, there was no guarantee that they would find a seller who was 100 per cent honest with them about the vehicle they were trying to re-sell.

Cars24 addressed all these issues. It put thousands of cars online and provided customers with all the information they would potentially need about the vehicles on offer, such as how many kilometres they have run, how old their engine is, how good their tyres are, and everything else there is to know about them. Since all of this was online, customers could also filter the offers according to their budget and specifications.

You choose the car you like, book a test drive, and buy the car only if you actually like it. Even after that, you have a seven-day return policy, should you face any unforeseen issues. These are all features you get only on big e-commerce platforms like Amazon or Flipkart, and they sure are not in the business of selling cars.

Additionally, a car is a substantially big purchase. It cannot exactly be compared with buying a t-shirt online. So, the online platform also gave the company the option to offer financing services within it. Suddenly, buying a second-hand car became easier for the common man.

'The output alone is not a true measurement, the amount of input that went in is equally important.'

When Vikram was asked what qualities one should look for in a co-founder, he said it all boiled down to only two factors. You should have mutual faith and a huge amount of respect for each other. Otherwise, there is no fixed formula.

It is also a given that you may screw up, and so may your co-founders. And that is fine. As long as they are giving inputs to the best of their ability, lower output can be overlooked. Things take time to work out. As they say, Rome wasn't built in a day.

'It really comes down to whether the person believes in you and the idea.'

Finding the right co-founders is not what makes a start-up successful. It only helps you establish a very strong foundation for it. You need a team of talented and reliable people who see eye to eye with you. Skills are secondary, belief and trust are what will lead your idea to fruition.

Find people who share your vision and who understand the nuances of the problem you are trying to solve; people who are passionate about bringing your idea to life. That's what makes a team strong. You'll face one problem after another on your journey, and building a team that enjoys the bumpy rides seals your start-up's success.

How Vikram and his team did that is by literally going through their Facebook friends lists and filtering out people they found could be a good fit for Cars24. They realized that many of these friends and acquaintances were actually interested in joining their venture. They interviewed a lot of people, who in turn referred them to more people, and the cycle went on. In this way, they ended up building the big and reliable team of over 8000 employees that they have now. Vikram says that although it took a lot of time to build such a team, every second of it was worth it.

'If you let what other people think of you bother you too much, then by definition, it becomes very hard to be an entrepreneur.'

People will always have opinions about you. Some might agree with you, some might disagree, but very few, whether they agree or disagree with you, would choose to stand by your side. The point isn't that you should not listen to what people have to say but that you have to focus on both the good and bad opinions, the bad even more. In criticism, you will find the flaws you need to work on.

'Anything good in life is challenging,' says Vikram. Being mentally and physically fit is hard; you have to work out every day and stay away from things that can affect your mind in a negative sense.

If these things were not so hard to achieve, would his team still feel their work is equally good and rewarding? Vikram tends to think otherwise, and he is probably right. And this is exactly why building a start-up is so hard because the outcome is as rewarding as it gets. If you are someone who enjoys building, you must enjoy the hardships and challenges that come with it too.

Petrol pumps fuelled their first set of customers.

When they were starting out, the Cars24 team's plan was to sell cars to customers. But the problem was, where would they get these cars? They realized that the supplies were with the sellers and that those sellers were individuals.

To find them, they started visiting petrol pumps. They did some calculations and found out that one out of every forty people who come to the petrol pump was a potential seller. They started talking to them, and the individuals they spoke to agreed to sell their cars on their platform. But the question was, what would be the selling price?

To figure out the price they went to some dealers and asked them how it was calculated. They realized there were too many factors that needed to be weighed in while calculating the value of a second-hand car and decided to leave it to the dealers themselves.

They added these dealers to a WhatsApp group. And whenever they found a potential seller they informed the dealers in the group, who then quoted their different prices, which were conveyed to the sellers. Cars24 ran on a WhatsApp group for over a year. Soon the team realized that a WhatsApp group would not suffice anymore and decided to build a dedicated platform.

'Do you really need to raise money? Do you know how to use that money? Spend that money?'

A common mistake, Vikram says, is that many new founders make is to keep raising money, in one round after another. Raising more money does not necessarily mean immediate success, but the founders sure end up diluting their stake in their company more than they should. As a young entrepreneur, you should never be tempted when you see many rounds of fundraising another start-up gone through.

Instead, you should see how much money you currently have and how much more you need, and map out how you intend to spend it. Raising more money that you do not really know how to spend efficiently is not going to help you in any phase of your start-up.

This is not to say that having more funding is bad. It is good. It gives you a safety net and proves to the world that people actually believe in your idea enough to invest money into it. It is something that increases your authority, but you should not raise funds just for the sake of it. Do it only if you need to.

'We believe in building a culture of openness, of honesty.'

Vikram says that for the last six years, he has tried to build a company culture that is honest, transparent and fluid. It is a place where people can be free to voice their opinions, even criticize others and disagree on the paths they need to take towards their destination.

But what they should never do is disrespect another. As your start-up grows, a lot of people come and go. So, it is important to build a culture where people are happy, even if they are leaving.

'Most people have their own fascination with a car.'

For an Indian, it is a moment of pride when a car is bought, but at the same time, buying one can make for a very painful experience. With Cars24, Vikram believes that the experience of buying a car is enriched by at least 1,000 times as compared to buying one offline.

'Irreversible decisions are more impactful than reversible decisions.'

Reversible decisions are like trying out a new restaurant; if you don't like it you don't need to visit there again. But irreversible decisions are like quitting a job—you can't get the same one back.

But what does that mean in business? Let's say you decide to raise more money for your idea. Once it is raised you cannot wake up the next day and return it, can you? You raised the money, so you have no other option but to invest yourself in scaling or growing your business. You cannot reverse this situation.

Your marketing strategy, on the other hand, can keep changing. You can experiment with new marketing tactics and put a stop to the ones that are not working well. It is completely reversible.

Almost every decision that is low on impact would be highly reversible. 'I just completely avoid such decisions,' says Vikram. Having the power to make many decisions as a co-founder might make someone believe that they are in control. But that is rarely the case, so never confuse one with the other.

Irreversible decisions, on the other hand, carry a much greater impact and force you to come out of your comfort zone and drive the decision to the finishing line.

Vikram also points out that the employees of every department at his company would make the argument that they work harder than those of the next department. For example, the sales team would always blame the marketing team for not giving them good leads for conversion, while the marketing team would blame the sales team for not being able to convert the leads they had generated after hours of hard work.

That is exactly the kind of malice Vikram tries to erase from the work culture of Cars24. He himself tries to stay away from it as much as possible. The thing he tells his team to always remember is that despite their differences they are the same team, working towards the same goal.

'Despite what most co-founders believe, fear is also an essential factor in any start-up's success.'

Fear of failure is a powerful motivator for many people and it can play a crucial role in a start-up's success. When faced with the possibility of failure, individuals are often pushed to work harder and think more creatively to find solutions and overcome obstacles. This can lead to new ideas and innovative solutions that might not have been considered otherwise.

Additionally, fear of failure can also serve as a reminder of why the founders decided to start the business in the first place. It can help to remind founders of their goals and aspirations and keep them focused on what they want to achieve. This can also lead to a renewed sense of determination and perseverance, which can be essential for success in the start-up world.

It is also important to note that embracing the fear of failure and not being afraid to take risks is key to a start-up's success. Entrepreneurship inherently involves a lot of uncertainty and risk, and the ability to navigate these challenges is what separates successful entrepreneurs from those who fall short.

'I don't think I have had to sacrifice anything.'

Vikram seems to have a unique perspective on the subject of sacrifices made by founders in building their start-ups. Unlike many other co-founders, who may view sacrifices as a necessary component of building a successful business, Vikram does not see it that way. Instead, he finds so much enjoyment in his work that the idea of sacrifice never enters his mind.

This outlook is likely a reflection of his passion for his work, which allows him to focus on the positive aspects of building a start-up rather than dwell on the potential negative consequences. Additionally, it may also reflect his confidence in his abilities and his belief in the potential success of his venture.

Vikram very openly says that he feels super-privileged in life. This attitude allows him to not feel the pressure of the trade-offs that most start-up founders feel they have to make. He sees himself as privileged and therefore doesn't feel that he is sacrificing anything for the sake of his venture.

While sacrifices may be a common reality for many start-up co-founders, Vikram's unique perspective on the subject highlights the importance of finding enjoyment and fulfilment in one's work. It also shows that success can come in many forms and that not everyone has to make the same sacrifices to achieve it.

Even if you have to make some sacrifices as a young entrepreneur, remember:

'Passion trumps sacrifice when you want to build something big.'

When it comes to the one question that Vikram would have liked to ask himself had he been in our shoes, he says it's more of advice than a question. When we are young, we are often swayed by what others have. It is okay to take inspiration and ideas from others, but in the end, we have to detach from envy and focus on what we want for ourselves. Instead of getting jealous, start getting inspired!

3

CoinDCX

Start-up Name	CoinDCX
Headquarters	Mumbai, Maharashtra, India
Sector	Cryptocurrency, Software
Founders	Sumit Gupta and Neeraj Khandelwal
Founded	2018
Valuation	$2.15 billion (April 2022)
Website	www.coindcx.com

About CoinDCX

CoinDCX is a cryptocurrency trading site, which is famous as one of India's biggest cryptocurrency exchanges. The company earned unicorn status by raising $90 million on August 10, 2021, and turned into India's first unicorn crypto startup. The business is focused on developing cross-

border financial services that ensure a smooth and continuous flow of resources.

—StartupTalky

Sumit comes from a very humble background. He was born in a small town and moved to a city when his father got a government job. He also moved from a Hindi-medium school to an English-medium one. The real turning point in his life came when he joined IIT Bombay, which turned out to be an eye-opener for him. He was surrounded by extremely smart people and got a taste of the real world.

Before IIT he had led a pretty simple life. The only things he had to worry about were studies and getting good grades, nothing else. He considers himself lucky to have experienced very different situations in life. There was a point when the family did not have enough resources to meet their needs, then a phase when they could just about meet their needs, and still another when they felt satisfied with what they had. These life experiences teach you to appreciate the things you have in life and also bring you the zeal to work for better things.

Throughout his life, Sumit has been a very curious person. It is safe to say that he had an entrepreneurial *keeda* from pretty early in life. When he was six or seven years old he started renting out video games. The intention wasn't to earn money. But that activity made him realize the importance of identifying the needs of people and seeing if one can make a business around it.

'At the very core, what you need to solve for is what people want.'

And if you want to turn it into a bigger business, just solve it at scale and do it way better than anyone else can. According to Sumit, those are some of the guiding fundamental principles in his life. You need to understand that nobody will give you money for nothing; you need to give them something of value. It's all about problem-solving. You do a business, you face a lot of challenges, you solve them, and you move forward.

Sumit met his co-founder Neeraj while preparing for IIT JEE in Kota. They became good friends and kept in touch. It was 2016 when they actually got together and found out that the Indian market is far behind some of the other countries in terms of innovation in the fintech space. So, they made a beginning by getting to understand the problems in that space.

They had some experience in the field and found that people did want to invest but there was no easy way to do it. The complexities of the process were becoming a hindrance. So, they decided to simplify this process. They never thought their venture could turn into a unicorn. That never really was the plan, it just happened.

They didn't build CoinDCX after looking at the market. They did it by being indifferent to it. They knew there would be ups and downs along their journey, but they were building for what the venture would eventually become. They were building the business when others in the same domain were shutting theirs, because of their conviction that their business had potential.

Sumit believes that it is valuable to see if you can identify patterns and predict what will happen in the future, what your thesis is. Hold on to your conviction, work towards it, and if it turns out to be true, you'll get rewarded. And in Sumit and Neeraj's case, their conviction really proved right.

Sumit believes that one of the highly underrated skills is the ability to understand people. When you talk to people you understand what drives them. There are some people who have a founder mindset, and there are others who have an employee mindset—both of which are fine. A founder mindset is when you see a problem, you go ahead and solve it. You take ownership of things. It does not necessarily need to be a business problem; it can be an employee's personal problem too. As a founder or a leader, you need to try to solve those problems too. You need to create a bond with your team and try to take them forward.

'Think like a CEO!'

Skill sets are overrated; they can easily be acquired. When hiring people, you should see if they have a problem-solving mindset, if they are driven and will take ownership of what they do. You need to find people who have the ability to evolve. They see what's going on around them and in the world and adapt accordingly.

Everyone at CoinDCX thinks like a CEO. This is one of their core values. When everyone in a company takes ownership, thinks like a CEO and is aligned to the same goal, the company grows really fast.

The bull run of the crypto market ended in 2018, so Neeraj and Sumit had to start from ground up. They created a small community of people and asked them for feedback. At that time, they were a team of four, and they started analysing the feedback to see if they could actually build something from ground up. That has been the core of the company—its people are very close to their customers, and this helps them understand what the customers actually need. And this in turn helps them grow.

'Culture should not be one size fits all. It is a derivation of your circumstances.'

Neeraj believes that the culture of a company is often defined by the circumstances. For a company to succeed, the mindset of its people must be aligned. The crypto space is very volatile and things can change and fail overnight. A team in the crypto space needs to be very resilient and persistent. They can't get demotivated by the downs. The culture for such a team should be built in such a way that the people accept that ups and downs will keep happening and they have to move forward regardless of them.

Neeraj says it is not in Sumit's or his nature to force people to work hard. They never force anyone to work hard. At the same time, they never entertain people who don't work hard. So, the people who succeed at CoinDCX are the ones who work hard on their own. This fosters a sense of ownership because people have to own what they do and work hard out of their own passion.

'Whether you build a culture or not, it will be built automatically.'

The culture of a company depends on the nature of the founders and their working style. So, it is the founders and the whole team that typically set the culture of your company, irrespective of what charter you may have.

Talking about fear of failure, Sumit believes that while building a start-up you are ultimately investing. It might work, or it might not, but at the end of the day it is an investment. Whenever you are starting up, it is important to be aware that there is a possibility that it may not work. While having confidence is good, you should also look at your venture in a complete and holistic way.

Although they have faced multiple failures at CoinDCX, the team knows what they are building. Sumit believes that the possibility of failure always exists, and it is natural to have fear of failure, but at the end of the day people should acknowledge the fact that they can fail, and then only will they be able to succeed.

Sharing their fundraising experience, Sumit says that it was very different from those of other start-ups. When they were starting up, people were very sceptical about investing in crypto, so in the beginning, the founders had to put their savings into the business in order to run it. They took some very calculated risks along the way and continued to do so.

'Fundraising is an art.'

Before you become a unicorn, a lot of effort goes into convincing people as to why they should invest in your business. You have to convince them about what exactly you are building, show that you are committed to it, tell them what the problem is and then prove to them, mathematically, how it can become a big business. Only if they are convinced will they give you their money.

What worked for CoinDCX, according to Sumit, is the fact that the team had always had innovation in their DNA. Whenever they do something, they do it differently and much better than others. They have always been persistent and they have always figured things out along the way.

'You can't build a fintech business without building trust first.'

In a fintech business, it is very important to gain the trust of the people. You cannot gain it on day one or even in a few months, but if you are there in the market providing the right value, fulfilling the needs of the customer, and have been around for a long time, then people start trusting you.

So, had Sumit and Neeraj been in our shoes, what question would they have liked to ask themselves? Sumit says he would have asked, 'Are you having fun?' When you are building something, he says, it is an endless road, so it's very important to have fun while doing it. If you are not enjoying it, you will run out of energy. No matter where you are in your life, you must ask yourself:

'Are you having fun?'

4

Dailyhunt

Start-up Name	VerSe Innovation Pvt Ltd
Headquarters	Bengaluru, Karnataka, India
Sector	Media and Entertainment
Founder	Virendra Gupta and Umang Bedi
Founded	2007
Valuation	$5 billion (April 2022)
Website	www.verse.in

About Dailyhunt

Dailyhunt, the local language content discovery platform, comes under the umbrella of VerSe Innovation, along with India's first short video platform, Josh. VerSe Innovation is an Indian local language technology company that was founded in 2007 with the goal of bridging the urban-rural digital divide in the country. From its inception, the company was heavily focused on leading-edge technological development and sought to be at the forefront of innovation in the consumer-facing Internet business.

As the Internet became more accessible, there was practically no content aimed at people who only spoke only the local Indian languages. Even something as simple as the news was not available to them on the Internet in their own language. VerSe Innovation has successfully bridged that gap with Dailyhunt and Josh. Through Dailyhunt, VerSe Innovation has tapped into the local language news, content and infotainment market that allows users to discover, engage and socialize with local language content. With Josh, VerSe Innovation has ventured into the lucrative short-form video market and is playing a key role in empowering regional creators from Bharat while contributing to the development of India's creator economy.

The co-founders of VerSe Innovation, Virendra Gupta and Umang Bedi, are very interesting people. How they met, how they became friends and how they eventually embarked on a journey to become one of the driving forces of India's digital transformation is a story to tell.

'Naukri chodo, vyapaar karo!' [Quit your job, start your own business!]

Umang comes from a middle-class family in Surat. While growing up he felt that his father had already sketched out his entire life's road map for him. From IIT to Harvard to getting a management job and retiring as a board member of some reputed company, the vision was all set. But life, it seems, had different plans for him.

As a child, he once saw a billboard urging people to quit their jobs and start their own ventures. Seeing the families of the kids in his school, he soon came to realize that almost every Gujarati owned a business of some sort. He always felt that everyone looked down on his father for doing a regular job, even though he was doing exceptionally well in his field.

To this day, Umang carries his learnings from Gujarat with him. He says they came in very handy while he took ownership of a business himself.

By the time Umang reached college, he had already started two businesses. He was in Pune, a city widely famous as the Oxford of the East with more than 500 colleges. He started assembling desktop computers and selling them to these colleges, and his business did really well.

Against his father's wishes, Umang took a job on campus because he didn't at all want to pursue further studies. But after a few years of this, he did succumb to the pressure and went to Harvard Business School, where he did his MBA. After college, he worked in different managerial positions at Adobe and Facebook group, which is today known as Meta.

While it was a successful phase of his career, he didn't enjoy the corporate bureaucracy. And a day after he turned forty he decided it was time to resign. He had also gained a lot of weight and didn't feel good about himself, so he went into a complete transformation drive and promised himself he would not work for 'someone else' ever again.

Soon he met Virendra Gupta, the other co-founder of VerSe Innovation. They commenced their start-up journey together, eventually ending up building a behemoth unicorn. When they talked, they realized that they had been working on solving the same problem, but continents apart. While one was in the USA and the other in India, they had both been trying to bring information services onto digital platforms.

Virendra started providing information services over text in the late 2000s, but the business wasn't taking off and he was in a tight spot. He saw an opportunity when the world began shifting to Android and smartphones were becoming more and more common. So he shifted his service model and started News Hunt in 2007, which today is known as Dailyhunt.

The target was Bharat inside India—the local-language audience. That business soon took off and grew exponentially. After the smartphone revolution in India came the telecom revolution in 2016, when Jio took the entire market by storm. Suddenly the Internet became cheaper and accessible to every common man.

But the revolution also brought a lot of competition for Dailyhunt.

Someone advised Virendra to check out how Facebook was expanding its business in India. He arranged a meeting with Umang, who was heading the India and South Asia division of Facebook at that time. Umang was excited to meet him as he was at that time working on localizing Facebook for fifteen languages. And who better to teach him how to go about it than Virendra—someone who had already captured the local-language audiences successfully!

After Umang left Facebook, he started building banking software, but knew that his heart was not in it.

Umang and Virendra had bonded over similar interests and kept in touch. After almost two years, Umang decided to take a trip to Goa with Virendra. Virendra knew banking software wasn't for Umang. He made him realize that his heart wasn't in it and that he belonged in the digital world. He offered to join hands with Umang to build something together, something new, and that's how VerSe Innovation was born.

'Capability. Attitude. A deep sense of purpose in what we are doing.'

These are the three factors based on which Umang hires people into his organization. He believes that the people you on-board should be filling the gaps you have in your skill set. If you cannot do something well, you hire someone who can. Similarly, when you hire at the initial stage, the people you on-board also grow along with your start-up. So, the focus should be on hiring people who are deeply collaborative and passionate about coming together to achieve a common goal.

While hiring, Virendra reached out to people he had known for a long time, who would be a great addition to VerSe's growing team. He and Umang were trying to fill in the skill gaps they had, with new members who could take complete ownership of whatever they undertook to do. For this reason, they also hired a CFO as they both lacked the financial expertise to drive things forward.

'Business and valuation will never go hand in hand.'

Business and valuation are two concepts that are closely related, but they are not necessarily dependent on each other. Business refers to the activities and operations of a company or organization, while valuation refers to the process of determining the worth or value of a company or asset. While a business can operate without a formal valuation, a valuation cannot be performed without a business to value.

However, it is important to note that the success of a business and its valuation are not always closely aligned. A business can be successful and profitable, but may not be valued highly by investors or the market. On the other hand, a business may be valued highly by investors or the market, but may not be generating significant profits or may not be sustainable in the long term.

Dailyhunt went from being valued at $585 million to $1 billion, becoming India's first tech unicorn focused on local languages. It did not stop there. During the Covid pandemic, it grew at a very rapid rate, and in April 2022 raised a whopping $805 million on a valuation of $5 billion. Raising $805 million in one single round is insane! The start-up was very close to being called a 'Dragon', a company that has raised $1 billion in a single round. Companies like Uber, Airbnb and our very own Indian e-commerce giant Flipkart are some examples of Dragons. As of January 2022, there were only twenty-four Dragons in the entire world.

This $805 million round for Dailyhunt was possible because over thirty-five of the world's largest venture capitalists, like Matrix and Sequoia, invested in it. And it has not only raised funds from VCs but also growth capital from companies like Goldman Sachs, Sofina, Google and Microsoft.

'Getting investments depends on your ability to tell a story.'

As a new start-up founder, it is important to understand that investors are not necessarily entrepreneurs. While they may have the financial resources to invest in your company, they may not have the same level of understanding or passion for your business as you do. However, this does not mean that you cannot secure funds from them. By clearly communicating your vision and demonstrating your understanding of the industry and market, you can earn their trust and convince them to take a bet on your company.

One effective way to do this is by telling your story in a simple and concise manner. Avoid using complicated jargon or flashy PowerPoint presentations, as these can overwhelm and confuse potential investors. Instead, focus on clearly and effectively communicating the key aspects of your business and how it addresses a specific problem or opportunity in the market.

Virendra has immense confidence in his co-founder's storytelling abilities and even says, 'There is no better person to raise money in India than Umang Bedi.' And we completely agree with Virendra as we were very impressed with Umang's storytelling skills too! Moreover, his voice is very deep and sounds not unlike Amitabh Bachchan's.

It is very important to keep a positive relationship with your investors. As they have already shown their confidence in your company by giving you their money, they can also serve as valuable ambassadors for your brand. By keeping them informed about the progress of your company and demonstrating your ability to effectively utilize their investments, you can earn their continued support and build trust with potential investors.

'Every person in the organization should make a difference to the business.'

Empowering ownership within an organization is crucial for its success. This means giving every person in the company the opportunity and ability to make a difference in the business. When employees feel a sense of ownership and responsibility for their company's success, they are more likely to be engaged, motivated and invested in their work.

One way to empower ownership is by giving employees autonomy and decision-making powers. Virendra believes that this allows them to take charge of their own work and make decisions that will further the company's success.

'Make mistakes and then ask for forgiveness'—this is something Virendra heavily preaches to all of his workforce at VerSe Innovation.

Another way to empower ownership is by providing employees with the necessary training and resources to succeed in their roles. Additionally, providing clear communication and transparent information about the company's goals and objectives can help employees understand how their work fits into the bigger picture.

'We want to build a company that outlives its founders.'

Umang says he wants to build a company that outlives its founders. When it comes to building a company that can be sustained for decades, a clear vision and a focus on longevity are key. His vision is to create a company that will be remembered as a transformative force in providing information and engagement to users everywhere.

Umang advises new founders to be mindful of 'founderitis'—the 'founder's syndrome'—where the founder has a 'my way or the highway' approach to running a business, which can destroy a start-up. To avoid this syndrome, it is important to approach data dispassionately, and objectively evaluate what is working and what is not. Founders should also be open to considering alternative perspectives and be willing to reassess their core beliefs. Finally, it is crucial to listen to customer feedback, as this can provide valuable insights and help guide the direction of the business.

'Be ready to be constantly proven wrong in the market.'

Just because you have an idea, it does not mean that it is going to be absolute. Entrepreneurship is inherently risky, and it is important to be prepared for the possibility of failure. But failure does not mean that you just give up either.

Being open to being proven wrong in the market means that you are willing to adapt and change your approach. It means being willing to pivot and make adjustments to your business model if it is not working. It also means being open to feedback and constructive criticism from customers, partners and industry experts.

As a founder, it is important to understand that your idea may not be the end-all solution. It is crucial to have empathy towards your customers, shareholders and employees in order to truly understand their needs and perspectives. This empathy allows you to make informed decisions and put the right people in the right positions within the company.

'Empathy coupled with action and the fire to solve for a customer is of utmost importance.'

You must move fast; you must be paranoid. You must always believe you are at war but always listen to and keep taking feedback from your customers. Keep giving them more of what they like while constantly improving on everything they do not. Umang believes that you should listen not just to your customers but also to your most junior staff. They can help you understand what is happening on the ground.

Virendra and Umang are like *Sholay*'s Jai-Veeru; their friendship is one for the books. They don't miss any chance to pull each other's leg, but they also don't miss any chance to sing praises of each other. When we asked them our curveball question, Umang said he would have asked himself who the best person on earth was. And Virendra said he would have asked himself which person had had the most impact on his life. And their answers? No points for guessing—they were each other.

We wished this had been an in-person interview as we would have got to know Virendra and Umang even better, given their friendly attitude. However, even the virtual interview on Zoom was as good as an in-person one! We did not even realize that we had spent ninety minutes talking to them!

Virendra is proud of the growth that India has been recording the last few years. Thousands of start-ups have already been built, and there are probably a million in the pipeline. Large numbers of entrepreneurs and innovative companies are emerging in various industries. This is because of the three advantages that India has—a young population, increasing access to technology, and funding. All this has helped fuel the growth of the start-up ecosystem in India, and both Umang and Virendra want to see India at the forefront of the start-up world.

'India is the biggest start-up!'

5

DealShare

Start-up Name	DealShare
Headquarters	Bengaluru, Karnataka, India
Sector	E-commerce, Grocery
Founders	Vineet Rao, Rajat Shikhar, Sankar Bora and Sourjyendu Medda
Founded	2018
Valuation	$1.7 billion (Feb 2022)
Website	www.dealshare.in

About DealShare

DealShare is a social e-commerce start-up based in Bengaluru. It was founded in 2018 by Vineet Rao, Rajat Shikhar, Sankar Bora and Sourjyendu Medda, and turned into a unicorn in January 2022. It has *raised $165 million via a Series E funding round led by Tiger Global, Alpha Wave, etc.*

Vineet's parents were originally from Karnataka, but he was born in Jaipur. So he grew up in a diversified cultural milieu. He had a typical middle-class upbringing, going through the general struggles of life, like saving money and only spending as much as was necessary.

In 1996, he went to IIT Bombay, where he studied computer science. He believes he grew up in very interesting times, as that was the time when a lot of changes were happening in the technology world leading up to the tech boom. But at the time he graduated, the Internet bubble had burst and the market crashed. so He joined a Texas-based start-up called Trilogy. Vineet was in Texas for a while and returned to start the company's India operations.

Trilogy was a very good company, working on some very ambitious projects for some of the top Fortune 500 companies and had hired really good talent across the world. But after the dotcom bubble burst, the money people had invested in these ambitious projects got wiped out. So, in 2004, Vineet decided to join Microsoft in Seattle. At that time Microsoft was doing a great many ambitious projects. But it eventually had to put the brakes on them as they seemed to be going in directions that led to nowhere. It had to really zoom in and let go of these ambitious projects.

The first lesson Vineet learnt at Microsoft was in terms of what you should really be signing up for. While being ambitious is good, you should go about business with a reasonable amount of realism too. You should know what can really be achieved and how you are going to achieve that. There should be a reasonable amount of planning before you decide to jump into something.

While at Microsoft, Vineet had enrolled in a leadership programme and got to connect with senior leaders of various companies. He got to understand how disruptive technologies are built. These experiences provided him with learnings on what really made a product successful.

First, you have to figure out what exactly the problem is, why you are trying to solve it, whether it is a problem worth solving and whether it is going to create business value. Many problems are worth solving; for example, you see a lot of potholes on Bengaluru roads, and they are definitely a problem that anybody can take on to solve, but how will you make money doing it? These, he learnt, were the questions to be asked while trying to build a business.

He worked at Microsoft for over ten years before deciding to return to India and build something of his own.

It was hard for him to come back to India after having done a lot of different work for different clients, and then to figure out what could be done and where the opportunities were. He tried his hands at a couple of things before finally deciding to start DealShare.

'There are right problems, then there is the right time to solve those problems.'

Before starting DealShare, he talked to many entre-preneurs. He met entrepreneurs who were trying to solve problems in the smaller cities and not getting a lot of visibility. Some of them were doing really good work and picking on good problems, but most of them were solving problems purely out of passion. They were really not thinking enough in terms of whether it was the right problems they were addressing or whether it was the right time to solve those problems.

Vineet thinks that timing is also extremely important when it comes to solving a problem. In fact, he wanted to launch DealShare in 2014 itself, when he came back to India. He built a proposal, talked to a lot of people and did his research. But, eventually, he felt the timing was not right. There was absolutely no interest whatsoever among anybody—whether they were friends, successful entrepreneurs or venture capitalists.

But, just four years later, everybody was super-interested in exactly the same concept. So, timing also is very important. Vineet takes the examples of Facebook and Google to explain that. Facebook was not the first social network; nor was Google the first search engine. It was not as if their predecessors were bad creations or were run by bad teams. What worked for the likes of Facebook and Google was the timing of these companies, which was much better and much more aligned with the needs of the market.

Vineet believes that the consumerization of technology happened in the early 2000s. Consumers were defining what next thing technology should go ahead and build, and enterprises were going by that.

'Instead of a few enterprises deciding what the next technology should be, it's the five billion people who drive the decision.'

Ten years back, very few people in the world had really good-quality smartphones or access to the Internet, but today almost everybody has them. It is only going to get better going forward because now, instead of a few enterprises defining what the next technology should be, it is the 5 billion people who will be defining what need the next level of technology will fulfil.

Nowadays you see a lot of innovation happening in the country through start-ups. But between 2008 and 2018, when the first wave of start-ups happened, people in India were just trying to replicate global models. They picked models which were very well-defined and successful in the US, Europe or China and tried to solve the same problem for the Indian audience.

Although it worked well for some start-ups, it didn't really work for retail businesses. A lot of capital was poured into retail, but the businesses could not endure simply because the per capita income or consumption patterns in India were very different as compared with those in the West.

Indian consumers were hungry and they wanted change. Although retail channels did exist, they were highly unorganized. The supply chain was not optimized and there was a lot of wastage, and consumers were ultimately paying ridiculously high amounts for goods compared to their production costs. But organized retail solves these problems.

To provide what customers really needed, Vineet decided to focus on the basics. The motive was to bring value to consumers on the kind of products they already used but at a better price point and without spending a lot of money on marketing.

Once you start building your solution, you will fall in love with it and will try to make it work. So, instead of building a solution, Vineet decided he would let the solution evolve. He simply started procuring relevant items at a much better price than what was available in the market and started selling on WhatsApp instead of trying to build a technology or an application.

That was Vineet's initial model. He and his team used to hunt for good deals and sell on WhatsApp. They used to ask customers to bring in more customers in exchange for micro-incentives. And the model really picked up. Even before they had any website or app they were doing daily revenues of $200 (around Rs 13,000), and that too while they were operating in only one city, Jaipur.

With the increasing demand, Vineet knew they could not keep running their business manually if they want to scale it. So, they made a simple website and then the app, and within a month sales shot up to $2,000 a day from a mere $200—again, without their spending any money on marketing. Vineet believes that you need to find your own problems and try to solve them at the very basic level rather than copy somebody else's solution.

Vineet believes India holds huge potential. There is no shortage of problems or opportunities for someone who tries to pick out problems and solve them based on first principles rather than trying to see if somebody else has solved them somewhere else and whether that is going to work in India or not. In fact, in the majority of cases, that approach has not really worked and makes for a very capital-intensive game, simply because if you are copying somebody, then somebody else with a bigger bag of money can easily do the same and throw you out.

DealShare started with three founders—Sankar Bora, Sourjyendu Medda and Vineet Rao; Rajat Shikhar also joined them a little later. Medda and Vineet had grown up together in Jaipur and studied in the same school. Medda had very vast experience in the Indian retail ecosystem; Shankar, on the other hand, had been a part of various start-ups since 2004 and had handled operations. Together they built a very strong initial team. Shortly afterwards, Rajat joined them. He had headed products at various start-ups. They hired locally and set up the initial team in Jaipur itself.

'For your founding team, find people you can build a very strong bond with.'

When it comes to picking co-founders, Vineet believes there is no clear recipe. Ultimately, it depends on how you define yourself and what you are really looking for. For Vineet, it was important to have a very strong personal connection with his co-founders. He believes that when you have a very strong bond with your founding team and your core leadership team, the results are always going to be a lot better than if you had a team of people who have much better qualifications or experience on paper but do not share a strong bond with each other. In a start-up, people have to be ready to get their hands dirty and do whatever it takes to build it, and for that you need a strong bonding in place.

Vineet and the team did not have a casual attitude when they started; going back to jobs was not really an option for them. They would have worked at their venture until it succeeded; luckily, it did not take them much time.

When it comes to deciding whether it is time to take the plunge, to leave your job to start your business, Vineet thinks it all boils down to whether you enjoy what you are currently doing or not. If you are passionate about something and you find that passion in the work you're doing, there's no need to stop doing that thing.

For the first seven years, Vineet enjoyed the work he was doing at Microsoft, but after that, it became a little monotonous. He realized that he wasn't enjoying the work he was doing and he knew something had to change, otherwise frustration would set in. The work culture was still great, but he was just not feeling sufficiently challenged intellectually.

It is all about what makes you happy. If you are not enjoying what you are doing, whether it is a job or a business, you need to take ownership of that and change it. It might not happen overnight; it took Vineet five years, but if you are persistent and patient, it will happen.

'For becoming a billion-dollar company, it is not just about the problem or the right solution, it is also about the right team with the right balance.'

When it comes to raising funds, Vineet believes that because of the current condition of economies across the world, the business which has better access to capital will have more chances of success. The amount of capital you both need and get will depend on the problem you are solving.

If you just start running around chasing capital without having any proof point pertaining to the problem that you are trying to solve—whether it is even a problem worth solving or whether there is even a market for the solution— then it is going to be very hard to raise capital.

You have to ensure that all this work has been done. For example, even if you have picked a really good problem but do not have the right team members, nobody is going to invest in your company.

Coming to the company culture—at DealShare, the team celebrates a lot. They started by building a very problem-solving kind of environment, every day finding problems to solve and then fixing them. And every time they solve a problem, they celebrate. It is important to build an environment that is fun and enjoyable so that people do not become too stressed at work.

The other part of it is the bond they share. Since the founders had very strong bonds among themselves, this naturally percolated into the company culture too. Everyone at DealShare is very ambitious, very hardworking and has very strong integrity. These are the only three qualities the founders look for while hiring at DealShare.

If you want to validate your start-up idea, you need to talk to a lot of people, take inputs from them, conduct some introspection and do rapid pilots. You need to assign a budget to your idea and a time limit, in the sense that if it is not working by a certain time, you will pull the plug on it.

You should have a timeline in mind—for example, that within the first twelve months, you will at least have seed funding. If an investor does not even want to do seed funding in your business, then you need to evaluate if it is worth spending your time on this start-up. For the next ten years, it is going to be an asset-heavy game in India, so you will need capital and for that, you will have to dilute your stake in your start-up.

Do not dilute too much of your capital, but don't be dilution-sensitive either when you know you have to build an asset-heavy company. As an entrepreneur, your ultimate goal should be to create a sustainable and viable business.

Now comes the curveball that makes almost every entrepreneur pause for a minute—What would they ask themselves, had they been in our shoes? Vineet says he would have asked, 'What is the thing that made you start up a company?' And, funnily, he did not have an instant answer to his own question. And he thought for as long as two minutes to even realize that he did not have an answer to the question.

Eventually, he did surmise that it was the network effect that possibly played a very important role in encouraging him to start up. He did have that entrepreneurial bug since he was young, but when he saw his friends doing their start-ups, that bug kicked in again. Since he was not happy at his job, he started introspecting and realized that no job was actually going to make him happy. He did not know whether he was going to be successful or not, but he knew he just wanted to try.

'If you never try, you will never know.'

6

Eruditus

Start-up Name	Eruditus Executive Education
Headquarters	Mumbai, Maharashtra, India
Sector	Education and Training
Founders	Ashwin Damera and Chaitanya Kalipatnapu
Founded	2010
Valuation	$3.2 billion (August 2021)
Website	www.eruditus.com

About Eruditus

Eruditus provides executive education programs intended for mid-career professionals. The company's portfolio of customized and open programs are designed and conducted in alliance with global leading business schools in a range of formats, including short workshops spanning a few weeks, online programs, or complete modular sessions, enabling professionals to get access to relevant programs that help them get new knowledge and grow in their careers.

—StartupTalky

Ashwin grew up in Chennai in a proper South Indian family. No one in his family had ever started a business, but everyone gave great importance to education. This emphasis on education can clearly be seen in Ashwin's career and the fact that he started a venture in the education sector.

Eruditus was not the first start-up by Ashwin, but it was surely the one that made him really happy. The intention was clear from the very beginning—if he was going to spend the next ten years of his life pursuing an entrepreneurial journey, it should make him feel happy and fulfilled even if it did not go well. So Eruditus, a company that caters to education, was a really nice fit for him.

Being a chartered accountant who did his MBA from Harvard Business School, education was really important to Ashwin. He believes that where a person comes from affects their outlook on life. Education changes young people's lives, and he wanted to be a vehicle to facilitate that change.

If you are someone who has a slight interest in business and how things work, you would have definitely heard about product-market fit. Ashwin believes in the concept of 'start-up-founder fit'.

If he were to start a business in crypto or fintech and the business had been very successful, he still would not have felt fulfilled because those fields do not resonate with him and his values. So, given his value system and what he wanted to achieve in life, he, along with his co-founder Chaitanya, started Eruditus as an experiment in 2010.

Did they know it was going to become so big? No. Nobody really knows what will click. You just have a concept that resonates with you, that you believe in, and you start working on it to achieve success.

They had a great journey, but it wasn't an easy one. Even in 2015, after they launched their online arm Emeritus, it was hard to raise capital. Twenty venture capitalists rejected them and refused to invest as they did not see a viable business in it. But that did not deter Ashwin and Chaitanya from their vision to make executive education accessible to people on a large scale.

They not only made Eruditus a viable business but also made it a unicorn. How did they do it? They had a good vision for it, and what they needed next was a good team.

'The first point of hiring a great team is to recognize that the odds are actually against you, they are not in your favour.'

Everybody thinks they are hiring a great team, but more often than not they are wrong. The traditional way of hiring is to get a resume, screen it, conduct an interview of the candidate and check the references—and there is still only a 50 per cent chance, at best, of making a successful hire.

So, if you want to get better at hiring do not use the traditional method. Instead, go with the more non-conventional methods.

Being a start-up founder, the key people you hire should essentially be the people whom you have worked with or know through one or two degrees of separation. 'I didn't know Chaitanya, but my CMO at Travelguru, my previous start-up, knew him—one degree of separation—and had great things to say about him. And I trusted his judgement. And, thankfully, it worked out,' says Ashwin.

That was one way of finding good people, but this way is a little limiting. So, what is the other way? The other way is to look beyond resumes and interviews. You have to ask yourself if the person you are considering is a good fit for your company. And how do you do that? By getting people to work on projects.

'If I'm going to hire a marketing person, I'll ask the candidates to make a two-year marketing plan and show me how they would go about it. Now, you'll find two types of people. Some senior people might say, "I'm too senior for this." Excellent. Don't even consider them because they'll be a very bad fit for a start-up,' says Ashwin.

'The other kind of people are the ones who will roll up their sleeves and actually get things done. They might have different insights on how they will get things done, but they will. And that's really what you need—a peek into their brain to know how they think and operate—and that's your second-best piece.

'People often say, "People are very important, getting a team is very important." Sure, if you care about the success of your business, you need to spend a lot of time on people, especially if you are a founder. But some people do lip service to this. I often ask founders how much time they spend on hiring people. And their answer is mostly 10–15 per cent. But if people are the most important thing in a business's success, why not spend 60–70 per cent of your time on them?'

'You can be out there putting out fires yourself, or you can hire a very good person who makes sure that there is no fire at all.'

Most of the advice entrepreneurs give is about working hard for your start-up. The one piece of advice Ashwin gives to start-ups and founders is to work smart instead of hard. 'Spend 60 per cent of your time initially on hiring good people. Do you need a CMO? Finalize at least three good candidates. You can choose any one of them and they will be a good fit but in the initial stage of hiring, it is important to have options. If you don't, you haven't done your job well.'

Eruditus is an education start-up. Hiring a good set of people is hard for all start-ups, but being in the online education industry ten to twelve years back, convincing top colleges to work and collaborate with Eruditus to create certificate programmes was definitely harder.

Ashwin recalls how, back in 2010, every college had this question to ask of them: 'Why should we work with these two young guys who are saying they will do great things but don't have a track record to show for it?'

The obvious choice for Ashwin was to go to his alma mater Harvard Business School and try to convince them to sign up. And that was what he did. But, again, it wasn't an easy task. It took six years for Harvard to agree.

Luckily for him, his co-founder Chaitanya was more persuasive than he was. He was an INSEAD alumnus and had also worked there. So it shouldn't come as a surprise that INSEAD became the first college to come on-board with Eruditus. The second institute to do so was Wharton. This became possible because an INSEAD professor who used to teach a joint programme with Wharton put in a good word about Emeritus there.

'When a door shuts, I never think that a door has closed. I think, okay, this door is just a little open, I need to push it open some more,' says Ashwin. And this could be the one sentence that is a true testament to Ashwin and Chaitanya's conviction in their venture, considering that in the first five years of Emeritus, Ashwin and Chaitanya were able to on-board only one school each year.

It took a lot of time to convince the universities, but Ashwin doesn't consider that a bad thing. Universities have great brands and they are protective of them. Ashwin and Chaitanya had to earn their stripes and show they could be a good custodian of those brands. And, considering the fact that they were able to on-board over fifty schools by 2021, it's safe to say they have come a long way.

It all comes down to your vision, purpose and conviction. If you believe you have a larger mission than just building a company that will make money for you, you get that extra motivation required to survive the harsh early years.

'Why can't you be like your brother? Just take up a job.' Most, if not all, start-up founders get to hear some version of this remark from the people around them. After all, there is always some fear of failure associated with entrepreneurship.

How does one tackle this external scepticism and one's own internal fear of failure? It varies from culture to culture, says Ashwin. Silicon Valley is great in this regard, as people there have very little fear of failure. India, on the other hand, is still only getting there. 'I had an offer from McKinsey, NY, and I could have gone there. I had a student loan to repay, after all.' But at the end of the day, you have to be very clear about what failure is for you. What entrepreneurs do differently from others is to take the plunge and start. You are always going to be a failure as an entrepreneur if you don't even start.

There are many who try to continue at their regular jobs while conducting their business on the side. Such businesses are doomed to fail.

'The world is very different from what it was back when we started. It's somewhat acceptable now even if you start your business and it doesn't do well. This whole experience is not really a failure but a learning experience.' Having this 'failure' early in your career is a very helpful thing. You may go back to a large business, you may become a consultant, you may join back a family business that you were with, but you'll be so much better at it.

'I was twenty-six when I started my first start-up, TravelGuru, which was a travel-tech start-up. Fresh out of business school, I had never done anything in the travel space. I don't have a tech background and nobody in my family was an entrepreneur. I struggled, raised capital, grew to a certain level and experienced all the ups and downs that come with a start-up.

'My learnings from TravelGuru are one of the reasons why Emeritus is so successful today. I went through all those mistakes from the time I was twenty-seven up to maybe thirty-two. And so, when we started Emeritus and Eruditus, I had those learnings that I could imply. So, this company found the product-market fit much better. I made much better hiring decisions. I was able to raise capital at the right time. I knew that for the first five or six years we shouldn't raise capital. I had made that mistake before, and I wouldn't make it again. We always knew that, look, cash from customers is more valuable than cash from VCs. All of these mistakes that you make early . . . you can use to be more successful in the future.'

'In fact, there was a Stanford faculty who said, "Look, let's assume I have to invest in a so-called charismatic entrepreneur who's starting for the first time, and my alternative is a so-called failed entrepreneur starting up for the second time. I can assure you that a hundred times out of a hundred I'll bet on the second-time entrepreneur because he or she has much more experience than the first-timer."

'Successful entrepreneurs dream of things that other people can't see,' says Ashwin. 'When I was pitching to our venture capitalists in 2016, most of them said no, but I had a vision. So, really, entrepreneurship starts there—in the mind. If you strongly believe that you can do something and achieve something great, I believe the whole world will conspire to make it happen. Now, of course, you need to understand that you still have to make pivots, you have to move forward, cut back, but the first thing is you must have belief. That's the difference between an entrepreneur and somebody who's an entrepreneur (only) in their mind.'

But how did the learnings from a travel-tech start-up help in setting up an education start-up? Travel is a very different space. TravelGuru was against very large competitors who raised a lot more money than it did, and that too very quickly. The first thing Ashwin learned was that if you burn money every time you acquire a customer, that is a horrible business to be in because then you are always at the mercy of venture capitalists. And if there comes a situation where the funding stops, it becomes very hard to keep your business afloat.

When Ashwin started TravelGuru, he thought they would be the first ones in the business. But before they knew it there came competitors like Cleartrip, Goibibo, etc. If you have something that has a very low barrier to entry, it is going to be a problem for you, and that was a big learning for him. When establishing a start-up, you need to go for uncontested spaces. Your start-up should have some unique moat or something that others cannot easily replicate.

That was what Ashwin and Chaitanya did with Eruditus. The long-term trusting relationship with the universities they have has taken years to build, and this has become their moat. So, even if someday some super, super-well-funded company wants to go after that space, it is going to take them much longer than it did Eruditus, which would have the time advantage.

Eruditus' story is full of lessons for entrepreneurs. As an entrepreneur, you should take your time to find a space that is large and uncontested. Then find your co-founders and a team that can turn your vision into a reality, and your business into a success.

You will hear a lot of Nos on your start-up journey, especially from VCs. Each time you do it should increase your resolve to prove them wrong, just as it did for Ashwin.

You need to raise money but you also need to raise money from the right people at the right time. If Eruditus had raised money back in 2010 in order to scale, maybe it wouldn't be around still because it wouldn't have been a good partner to the universities.

One quality of venture capitalists is that they see so many companies that they're able to synthesize learning across a large set of data and pattern gauges and give you insights. The insight they gave Eruditus was that as long as it was classroom-based, which is what its first avatar was, it would not be able to scale. So, Ashwin and Chaitanya thought about going online much more deeply.

Knowing something and realizing it are two different things. Back in 2015 when Eruditus started, it was 90 per cent classroom and 10 per cent online. The team also knew that online was important, but when they got this feedback from everybody they realized that the strategic future of the company had to be online. They started focusing more on online, made investments, showed traction, and were able to raise capital and grow.

When you talk to investors you get to know a lot about different sectors. They can give you useful insights. Sometimes their feedback can help you pivot, but that's not a necessity. Sometimes, as an entrepreneur, you see certain things that nobody else does, and that is crucial for the creation of uncontested spaces.

At the same time, you should not be so attached to your idea that you cannot see the bigger picture. As an entrepreneur, you have to decide which of the options really makes sense for you.

In the beginning, Eruditus was a brand from India for India. Going online helped it also go global. The team realized that MIT, Wharton, Columbia, etc., were all global brands, so when Eruditus went online they saw students coming to the platform from all over the world. Today, 80 per cent of their students are from outside India, but 70 per cent of their employees are based in India. The education and exposure of the founders and the global experience of the founding team helped them become a brand from India for the world.

The successful part of their culture is this approach they refer to as 'box one, box two, box three'. Box one is about all the projects and initiatives they are doing today. It is about the current quarter and the current year. Box two is about what they are going to do next. But their culture is equally about box three, which consists of projects they are not doing today but want to three, five or ten years down the line. Between 10 per cent and 20 per cent of their projects are always for the future. Some of them will fail; in fact, many of them will fail, but one or two will become successful too. So, back in 2015, going online was box three for them, and it looks like they have checked that box, and how!

Now, an important question to ask is, would your idea become a start-up? You need to think about an MVP, that is, minimum viable product. MVP is like an experiment that you run. You need to start something and work on it. You can fail—that is not a problem—but even if you fail you will have data to show what works and what doesn't, and that will really help you move forward.

You might need to sacrifice a lot; after all, everything in life calls for sacrifice. But, instead of looking at what you are giving up as a sacrifice, if you look at it as prioritization, the approach becomes much more positive. Everything in life is about prioritization. Start-ups test your own personal resolve and resilience a lot. But once you go through that experience you learn how to deal with it.

There are highs and lows. So there are some really nice moments when you feel on top of the world. Like when Ashwin and Chaitanya landed university partners or some course did well, or some student came and told them, 'Look, I took your course and it changed my life'. As founders, these little instances made them feel wonderful. It gave their lives meaning.

But sometimes, some unexpected thing happens too and you're like, 'oh God, what am I doing?' So, a start-up is essentially a rollercoaster ride. A lot of things happen in life; you're not in charge of everything and so you have to let go. From the outside, you can be very ambitious, but from the inside, you need to be very modest. Once you have that internal modesty, prioritization becomes easier.

What would be the advice from a unicorn founder such as Ashwin to a young individual who is just starting out?

Ashwin strongly believes that in situations where everything is going well for you, you learn the least. When you put yourself in a tough situation, that is when you learn the most. So, as a young individual who is just starting out, you need to put yourself in difficult situations that can provide you with the maximum learning opportunities. Do not just keep going for safety.

Even if you do not have training in a particular field but you want to do something in it, you just need to go for it. A lot of times you might have been made to feel, either by yourself or by others, that you cannot do it. But if you believe in something you stay in it, and you stay the course. For Ashwin, that's the biggest difference between an entrepreneur and somebody who doesn't even start.

'The only way to be an entrepreneur is to be an entrepreneur.'

One question that Ashwin would like to ask himself is, 'If he had to write something on his own tombstone, what would it say?' He thinks everyone should ask themselves what their legacy is going to be. For him the determiner of his success would be how many lives he positively impacted with the things he did. Right now that number is around 1 lakh, but he is just getting started and wants to make it 10 lakh in twenty years.

After all, entrepreneurship is all about adding value to people's lives! It's not about the money you make, the fame you get, or the wealth you create! It's all about creating an impact!

Focus on value creation, and not on valuation.

Well, a special shout-out to Ashwin as he was the first of our entrepreneurs to agree to an interview with us! With that we got the confidence that we would be able to convert twenty founders if we were able to convert at least one. We are grateful to Ashwin for helping us achieve our dream of meeting twenty unicorn founders!

7

FirstCry

Start-up Name	FirstCry
Headquarters	Pune, Maharashtra, India
Sector	Online Baby Products
Founder	Supam Maheshwari
Founded	2010
Valuation	$2.7 billion (August 2022)
Website	www.firstcry.com

About FirstCry

FirstCry is an online-cum-offline brand providing a wide range of products for babies, children and mothers. The start-up was born out of a desire to solve the problem of millions of parents in India of not having access to the best brands and baby care products for their offspring. The product categories at firstcry.com comprise diapering, feeding and nursing, skin and health care products, toys, clothes, footwear, fashion accessories and much more.

Who can tell the unicorn Secret better than the man who has created not one, not two, but three unicorns? Supam is a serial entrepreneur who has created three successful and profitable unicorn start-ups in India: FirstCry, Globalbees and Xpressbees. However, he is not one to brag about his accomplishments, so you would not see him talking too much about them. We are extremely humbled and honoured that he agreed to give us an interview. Usually, he doesn't appear in the media as he doesn't like to be in the limelight. He places great importance on creating tangible outcomes rather than engaging in vain boasting. In doing so he does not think of himself as being modest; instead, he feels he is just being realistic. He may not talk much, but when he does he surely creates an impact. We were awestruck by his humility and authenticity as he answered all our questions!

Supam's story doesn't start with FirstCry. His journey began when he was shifted from a Hindi-medium school to an English-medium one. It wasn't an easy transition. He recalls how he had to write a leave application once and couldn't do it because it had to be written in English. Thereafter, he had to work really hard to feel a sense of belongingness.

When you come from a humble, middle-class background, you find out that there are two kinds of people—the haves and the have-nots. If you are among the latter, it can make you feel inferior and question yourself about everything.

He did his engineering and then got into IIM Ahmedabad for his MBA. But the entrepreneurship *keeda* didn't come after his master's qualification; in fact, it had always been there. He wanted to improve his life experiences and for that, he knew he had to create something of his own. He always dreamt big, and with time, his dreams just got bigger and bigger.

He had only known about manufacturing in his early childhood, so he wanted to do something in that field. And he thought doing engineering was the best way to go about it. At that time, everyone was doing an MBA, so he followed the herd and did an MBA too.

His academic years made him feel miserable. He was a practical person who was stuck in the world of theory. But he had to finish what he had started, so he went on to complete his MBA. After that, he joined PepsiCo, as he thought it would help him travel to different places. He did get to handle a variety of projects, participate in important decisions and deal with people in senior profiles. But once the operations were set up, there was a vacuum. He got bored and told the MD that he would be starting something of his own and hence moved to Pune.

From the very beginning, he knew he did not want to work for anybody. The games he used to play as a kid had instilled a competitive spirit in him. The goal was to win, but he knew he wanted to do it with a team.

Before starting something on his own, Supam consulted one of his seniors, who advised him to start an Internet business. And so he did. He looked for people with complementary skills and started BrainVISA back in 2000.

BrainVISA was an ed-tech platform that helped students with their entrance test preparations. The thing that didn't work out for him was that he was too early in the business. The dotcom bubble burst. Supam and his team were left with little money in their bank account and hence had to pivot. The platform's initial B2C model was changed into a B2B one as they realized that the market they were trying to penetrate didn't exist yet.

So they built a learning management system and shifted their focus from India to overseas. Once they did that they started making profits and never had to look back. After seven to eight years in the business, they sold the business and everybody made good money.

While working on BrainVISA, Supam had to travel a lot for business development. He loved to buy gifts for his daughter from the countries he visited. And he realized there was a lack of availability of quality products for children in India.

After BrainVISA, Supam and his team wanted to do something that could be scaled, and retail seemed like a good option to him. They ran their numbers, did their research and realized that people had to travel around 17 km to buy baby products in Pune, and even then they could not be sure they would find what they were looking for. Supam wanted to solve this problem. The market was fragmented, both on the demand and supply sides, and they had an opportunity to streamline it, as a result of which FirstCry was born.

FirstCry started in 2010 as a platform for selling essential products like diapers, lotions, oils, toys, etc. And at that time, their biggest competitor used to be Mom & Me, which they ended up acquiring in 2016.

What worked for FirstCry was the effort that has been put into figuring out the vision for the company. Supam believes that it is the most important part of a start-up. His team already had entrepreneurial experience from BrainVISA, and once they realized what their vision was, then it was all about execution.

Now that they had the vision and execution sorted, how did they acquire customers? Initially, it was all by word of mouth and organic Facebook reach. They were only focused on service, which resulted in positive word-of-mouth publicity.

'People with humble backgrounds have the capability to become long-term partners.'

In the initial days of FirstCry the entire team was working like an execution machine, and that is why it is very important to hire the right people. What did the founders look for in their initial employees? Having run one business, they knew that the two traits that are a must in an employee are a great attitude and passion. Competence is abundant in India, and if a person has the right attitude, he or she can learn things very quickly.

Finding good talent was never a problem, thanks to the brand equity that BrainVISA had created. Most of the initial set of people at FirstCry came from BrainVISA, including the co-founders.

'There's nothing called hiring a co-founder. It's marrying a co-founder.'

When it comes to co-founders, you can't 'hire' them. You hire employees who do process work; you can't hire co-founders or senior management because they are not your employees, they are your partners.

'Culture does not get created by putting up posters or laying down some value system.'

It is your relationship with your co-founders, senior management and employees that shapes the culture at your workplace. Your employees always look up to you, so you need to lead by example. Frugality and integrity are part of FirstCry's DNA, and it is by the founders setting a precedent that these qualities are imbibed by the team. And that's how culture in a company is built—**leading by example.**

'The fabric of culture actually binds everybody together.'

When you have a solid vision and a team that can execute that vision, you can face all challenges that come your way. There will always be challenges, but you will also be able to deliver on those challenges, thanks to the culture that you have created.

When it comes to seeking funding for a start-up, you need to understand that every case is different, every environment is different, and the risk profile is also different. There are no right and wrong ways, you do what works for you.

'It's crucial to see the vastness of the idea and the ability to add value to that idea in order to make a difference.'

There are different stages of a company's life cycle. If you are a young entrepreneur straight out of college or a dropout, then you might need the support of an angel. But before you reach that particular point, Supam advises thinking very hard about your idea and what you are really going after. Consider if the idea really drives you and is scalable. Consider what value addition an investor can make to transform your idea into a reality. For Supam, this is more fundamental than raising capital. If you have a clear vision, raising money will become easier, as then it will be all about execution.

If you have a mature idea and have established your credibility in the past, you can go for Series A funding. How big the cheque is going to be in Series A also depends on the maturity of the idea and the team. From Series B onwards, it is all about execution.

In India, it is easier to get funding for a Ctrl-C + Ctrl-V kind of idea, as VCs also need their safety net. Most of the ideas pursued by start-ups are not very different from each other, and it is in the execution that they would differ. India is a country with vast geographical and demographical differences, and it is your execution that can make your start-up work.

'In a world running on instant gratification, an entrepreneur should try to imbibe (practise) deferred gratification.'

If your only goal is to make money, then you are doing it wrong. It is not as if money is not important, but it cannot be your end goal. The bigger you become, the more challenges you will face. You have to be very sharp, you have to be very fast, quick, nimble, build relationships and keep delivering value. If you do so, investors will love you and Series C and Series D funding will become very easy.

'Raising capital is a journey in itself. When you build trust and deliver value to your shareholders and investors, it becomes easier for you to raise capital.'

Although Supam and the team have created three unicorns, that was not really the idea. Their aim was to solve problems that existed rather than to chase money. And Supam believes that when you don't chase money, money starts chasing you.

When you are creating something, something big, fear of failure is sure to seep in. But you cannot tell others about it; you have to live with it. You can share it with your partner or co-founders, but you cannot show that fear to others. Being an entrepreneur at the helm of a business, that is the risk you sign up for.

This is where having co-founders really helps. During the moments when you are feeling low, your co-founders become your support system and help you to rise. There may be pitfalls in between, but your partners are there to serve as a ray of hope and back you. And when you know you are being emotionally backed, you get the courage to rise and soar high.

Fear of failure can only be overcome by emotional strength. It is your partners' emotional strength and passion that can counterbalance your mind's negativity and help you cross that bridge.

As you age, your life will hold a different set of meanings from earlier. You are not just an entrepreneur; you're also a husband, a father, a son, a son-in-law and a friend. You have so many roles to play. In building a start-up, you might neglect some of them and they might become your regrets later, but as you grow in years you need to try your best to work on the things you earlier missed out on.

The one question Supam would have liked to ask himself is, 'Where do you draw your inspiration from?' He goes on to answer it as: 'What inspires me are some of the great stalwarts who have continued to inspire themselves. I don't know who inspires them, but I still get inspired by them.' His inspiration also comes from seeing happy faces around him. Seeing other people grow drives him. And he just wants to keep taking that to the next level.

'It's all about taking it to the next level. Except, the next level never comes.'

8

Fractal

Start-up Name	Fractal Analytics
Headquarters	New York, United States
Sector	Analytics, Artificial Intelligence
Founders	Srikanth Velamakanni, Pranay Agrawal and four others who have exited
Founded	2000
Valuation	$1.5 billion (January 2022)
Website	fractal.ai

About Fractal

Fractal Analytics is a multinational artificial intelligence firm that serves Fortune® 500 companies across areas such as consumer packaged goods, insurance, healthcare, life sciences, retail, technology and finance.

'"An honest businessman" is an oxymoron.'

This was something Srikanth's father used to tell him when he was growing up. His father worked as an electrical engineer for an oil company in Assam. He was convinced that businesses are corrupt and that his son should focus more on getting a decent job.

The pressure to be good in academics was, of course, part of Srikanth's life, and he grew up with the same critical views about business and entrepreneurs. He was certain he did not ever want to be an entrepreneur. Nor did he have the ambition to be one—or at least that was what he thought.

He studied hard and made his way to IIT Delhi, with hopes of building his career working for some big companies. He chose to do engineering because of his love for mathematics, and not because he ever aspired to be an engineer. He went on to do his MBA from IIM Ahmedabad.

In the following years, he worked for Australia and New Zealand bank, known as ANZ, and for ICICI. He enjoyed both these stints very much.

The Fractal story began when he was studying at IIM, even before he had begun to work. Narayana Murthy, founder of Infosys, had given a guest lecture at his institute and had talked about the conviction, values and ethics based on which he had founded his own company. For the first time in Srikanth's life, his entire perception of businesses was challenged.

He was inspired by the Infosys founder's unwavering commitment to his venture and realized that success in business could be achieved without compromising one's integrity. This was a new concept for Srikanth, who had always assumed that success in the corporate world was only possible through cut-throat competition and greed.

The other concern that he had was about how to raise the huge capital he would need for a business. But in the late nineties, new venture capital companies were just coming to India and it had become possible to raise capital through them. During the fledgling stages of venture capital in India, while opportunities were limited, funds were still attainable if you were determined enough.

Starting a company often involves a combination of factors, including opportunity, personal experience and personal drive. In the case of Srikanth, the Narayana Murthy talk and the advent of venture capitalists in India were the two episodes that played a role in inspiring him to start Fractal Analytics. Were it not for these incidents, it is possible that Srikanth's journey might have taken a different path and he might not have started the company.

'Great ideas are born by understanding the pain of users.'

Great ideas often stem from an understanding of the pain points of users. When you know what problems people are facing, you are better equipped to create solutions that will resonate with them. To ensure that your idea is impactful, you must consider both big and small ideas. As the market expands, even small ideas can grow into something much larger.

When evaluating your idea it is important to ask yourself whether it solves a problem better than the existing solutions. Does your idea offer a unique approach? Or does it provide a significant improvement over what is already available? This is what will set your idea apart and make it stand out in a crowded market.

'Getting into an IIT is an accomplishment, but it also humbles you.'

Getting into an IIT can be a significant accomplishment and bring the entrant a sense of pride and satisfaction. IITs are considered to be among the best technical institutes not only in India but also around the world. They attract students with high levels of academic ability and motivation. As a result, students who obtain admission to these institutions can feel a sense of achievement that they have made it to a top-ranked college.

However, Srikanth says that attending an IIT was also a very humbling experience for him. When students arrive on campus, they quickly discover that they are now among people who are much smarter than them.

They are surrounded by talented individuals who are equally motivated and driven to succeed as they are. This can be both challenging and inspiring, as students are pushed to perform at the highest levels and grow both intellectually and personally.

Srikanth also says that the friends he made in college are still a vital part of his life. Not just that, but many of his college friends are involved with Fractal in one capacity

or another—some as investors and some as clients or even
advisers.

'Focus on building better relationships in B-schools.'

Many individuals attend the Indian Institutes of
Management (IIMs) with the primary goal of securing
a job rather than to study there for the sole purpose of
education. However, this focus on achieving success
can lead to a highly competitive environment, causing
individuals to prioritize their personal and academic goals
over their relationships.

Srikanth is critical of this attitude, as he believes that
the relationships formed in business school can prove to
be valuable in the long term, even twenty and twenty-
five years later. It is important to strike a balance between
personal and professional growth and maintain healthy
relationships during one's time in business school.

'If you have a deeply trusting relationship and someone is complementary to you, that's the best co-founder you can get.'

In addition, having a co-founder who complements your
skills and expertise can bring a unique dynamic to the
partnership. In Srikanth's case, the person he reached out
to when starting Fractal was his B-school classmate Nirmal
Palaparthi, who always wanted to be an entrepreneur.
Unlike Srikanth, who never wanted to be one, Nirmal was
certain he did not want to be anything else.

The second person he reached out to for his founding team was Pranay Agrawal, who already had a very established career. Srikanth didn't expect him to say yes to joining his team, but to his surprise, Pranay said yes immediately.

Srikanth advises that you should look for qualities in partners that you lack. If you are someone whose expertise lies on the commercial side of the business, you should find a co-founder who can take care of the technical aspect of it. If you are a CEO, you should find a CTO. Even if you share similar traits as partners, you should discuss diversification and try to branch out into different roles.

'Break the chicken-and-egg situation.'

When it comes to acquiring the first customer for any start-up, Srikanth says it is very comparable to the infamous chicken-and-egg situation. You might be capable of solving the greatest problem facing a potential customer, but since you have no credibility, why would they believe you?

You have to recognize that you're not the only one solving a problem for a customer, they are also solving one for you. They are giving you the golden opportunity of turning them into your first customer. It's a two-way street.

You can't just walk up to a person and ask them for their money. You have to convince them that they are getting equal value out of it. Fractal's first customer turned out to be Srikanth and Pranay's ex-employer, ICICI Bank. ICICI was preparing to build its own branch of financial services in India, but it did not have the expertise for it.

The bank was building mathematical models to estimate risk. Srikanth reached out to an IIT Delhi classmate of his, who worked at ICICI and told him that Fractal had the expertise to build these models and personalize them for India. Until that point, ICICI was taking global models from a USA-based firm, which would not have been very effective in India.

The problem was, Fractal was a fresh start-up, so why would ICICI even give them a chance? So Fractal offered to do it for free. All they asked in return were some testimonials if they did a satisfactory job. They did more than that. They built a product that reduced the time for a customer to get a loan to just thirty minutes.

If you went to a store to buy an expensive TV, within thirty minutes you would get a loan and the TV would be yours. Thirty minutes for a simple loan might sound like a lot in 2023, but Fractal did it all the way back in 2001.

This is how ICICI Bank became their first customer. Now that they had testimonials, Fractal reached out to other banks. This time they did not have to offer anything for free. Soon they had on-boarded various banks, HDFC being the biggest of the bunch. Fractal was building on the trust they had built with ICICI.

'If your start-up has the right purpose and inspiration, the right people will find you.'

Fractal was very particular about who they hired in their team. But they also wondered why anyone would want to join them. They were not offering attractive salaries; neither were they among the big names in the industry.

One day an acquaintance of Srikanth's from IIT Madras reached out to him. He was interested in the work Fractal was doing in risk modelling and creative risk management, and wanted to be a part of the team. When Srikanth and his co-founders interviewed him, he turned out to be a great fit and became the first employee they on-boarded.

'The best talent is actually interested in you not because of your reputation as a company but because of the size of the problem that you're trying to solve,' says Srikanth. One by one, talented and interested people kept reaching out to them, and soon they had built the initial team at Fractal.

'If you want money, ask for advice. If you want advice, ask for money.'

'Fundraising is like dating,' Srikanth says. Looking for an investor is very similar to searching for a dating partner. If you are too desperate for either, it is going to blow up in your face. Convincing investors to fill your start-up's pockets with their money is already hard. If you show your desperation, there is a high chance that they won't give you any. The more desperate you are for something, the less your chances of getting that thing.

What you should do is talk to investors and discuss your ideas; tell them about your plans for scaling it and making it a profitable business. If they believe you, they will happily give you the money without even your asking for it.

Srikanth also believes that it is always better to raise more money than less. Dilution is a natural part of any start-up, and you will be giving up a certain amount of equity, no matter how much money you raise. If you have more money you will have a greater range of options when it comes to experimenting with your ideas.

'I fundamentally believe that entrepreneurs should focus on making a bigger pie rather than having a higher share of a smaller pie.'

Contrary to popular opinion, Srikanth believes that dilution is not as bad as people say it is. What you need to remember is that investors do not want to build your company. They are giving you their money so that they can make a return on their investment. So, why not build it as big as possible?

You should care less about how much control you have over your company and focus more on how many times you can grow it by utilizing your current funds in the right way. The people who make the initial rounds of investment in your idea are in it for the long game. They want a huge return on their investment, possibly 50x to 100x. That is why they are giving you their money when you haven't even built your company. So, when it grows, their money grows with it too.

It is also important to treat your investors right. If you have differences with them, work towards a resolution. If they want an exit, give them the returns on their investments and let them leave with respect. It is important to create healthy relationships with your investors. Your new investors will always see how you treated your previous investors and make their decisions accordingly.

'Culture is what is happening in the company when no one is looking.'

Srikanth recalled the early days of Fractal when there were only twenty parking spots for the team, and it was on a first-come-first-serve basis. Even Srikanth did not have a slot reserved for himself, which really frustrated his driver. So, his driver put up a poster at a parking spot that said that it was reserved for his car.

One of Srikanth's colleagues came up to him one day and said he too would like a reserved parking spot. Srikanth was not aware of what his driver had done, and he went down and tore the poster down. It is all about maintaining a sense of equality.

Srikanth has created a culture of transparency where anyone can ask a straight question and expect a 100 per cent honest answer.

'AI wasn't even a thing when Fractal began.'

In today's era of the Internet and technology, AI is all the rage. It is all people can talk about. Fractal's entire model was around AI, only that the term was not very prevalent back then. They also had to face a lot of challenges because of it, as early movers in any industry do.

Just like a lot of other start-up founders, Srikanth believes that Fractal should stand the test of time, and cares less about the profits of the next quarter. Rather, he is focused on Fractal's long-term future.

His vision is to create a company that sustains itself no matter who leaves or who joins. Constantly reinventing the company structures as times change is the key to achieving longevity for any organization. If you do not evolve, you cannot live.

'Entrepreneurship is all consuming.'

Entrepreneurship is a demanding pursuit that calls for strong passion and commitment to success. It is not just about being your own boss or making more money. Those are just bonuses that come along with it. To be a successful entrepreneur you must have a deep-rooted passion for your business and a strong drive to see it grow.

Being an entrepreneur means your start-up is your top priority. Every decision you make and every action you take must be focused on growing your business. This can be all-consuming and require a great deal of time and effort. However, for those who are truly passionate about their business, all this is a very small sacrifice to make.

It is important to remember that as a founder of a company, your family and your workforce together become your family. You have to give proper time and attention to both. Luckily for Srikanth, his family is already very invested in Fractal, which makes his day a little easier.

Being an entrepreneur requires a unique combination of skills and mindset, and one of the most crucial attributes to have is an optimistic outlook. Optimism is the fuel that drives you to keep pushing forward, even when faced with setbacks and obstacles. It helps you maintain a positive attitude and gives you the mental strength to keep going. Additionally, optimism can also help you build resilience, which is crucial for success in any venture.

Another important skill for entrepreneurs is the ability to sell. Whether you are trying to win over clients or investors, the ability to communicate your story in a compelling way is essential. This requires a strong understanding of your target audience as well as the ability to articulate your vision and values in a way that resonates with them. The ability to sell is not just about making pitches or presentations but also about building relationships and establishing trust with your potential customers and investors.

The one question Srikanth would have asked himself, had he been in our shoes, was, 'How do you learn?' Everything is changing all the time; you need to evolve with the evolving world in order to succeed. According to Srikanth, how you learn every day and whom you learn from are very important.

Learning is an ongoing process and a key aspect of personal and professional growth. As an entrepreneur, it is especially important to stay informed and up-to-date with the latest developments in your industry and the world. This requires a strong commitment to continuous learning, as well as the ability to adapt and evolve with the times.

According to Srikanth, one of the best ways to enhance your learning is to read a lot of books. Reading not only expands your knowledge but also helps you develop new perspectives and insights. Another effective way to learn is by engaging in intellectual discussions.

By having meaningful conversations and debates with people who challenge your ideas, you are exposed to different perspectives and ways of thinking. This can help you refine your ideas and expand your knowledge in new and exciting ways.

Additionally, intellectual discussions with others can help you develop critical thinking and problem-solving skills, which are essential for success as an entrepreneur.

It has been twenty-three years since Srikanth started Fractal, and he wants it to keep growing for years to come.

'I want Fractal to be an institution that stands the test of time and remains relevant long after I am gone.'

9

Good Glamm Group

Start-up Name	Good Glamm Group
Headquarters	Mumbai, Maharashtra, India
Sector	D2C
Founder	Darpan Sanghvi, Priyanka Gill and Naiyya Saggi
Founded	2021
Valuation	$1.2 billion (November 2021)
Website	www.goodglamm.com

About Good Glamm Group

Founded by Darpan Sanghvi, Priyanka Gill and Naiyya Saggi, the Good Glamm Group is South Asia's largest content-creator-commerce conglomerate. It brings together the group's innovative and fast-growing beauty and personal care brands, powered by the group's proprietary digital ecosystem of content and creator assets. The Good Glamm Group umbrella has three key divisions: Good Brands Co, Good Media Co and Good Creator Co.

'At heart, I am a brand builder, and that comes from the innate excitement creative brand building gives me.'

Darpan Sanghvi, founder of the Good Glamm Group, comes from a very entrepreneurial family. Even as a ten-year-old, he used to sit with his father and look up the stock prices of companies. His dream was always to be an entrepreneur. As he grew up, he started trying to figure out how to make that dream a reality.

He started his first business in 1999, at the age of nineteen. It was a dotcom business, at the time when dotcom was booming. As a youngster, he saw some amazing stories of dotcom business success, got fascinated by them and jumped into a dotcom business himself. He had no clue what he was doing, but at age nineteen, he had his own dotcom business.

Although the business went nowhere, he got some press and media, and the founders of baazee.com, an online marketplace, invited him for an interview. So, at nineteen he started working for baazee.com.

He did that for a year, and then, like every good Indian kid, did his engineering. He finished his engineering course and then went abroad for his MBA. He went to ESADE business school in Barcelona for a year and then to the University of Texas at Austin for a year.

Post his MBA, he worked for a chemicals company for a couple of years and then began his second start-up in New York City, which was in the children's fitness space. He ran it for a year, but could not pull it off. Unable to raise capital, he put all the funds he had saved from three years of working and spent it in a single year. Then, when he ran out of money, he decided to move back to India and start looking for something here. He was now twenty-eight.

It was not until Darpan was thirty that he stumbled on an entrepreneurial opportunity that turned into something meaningful.

'An innate quality of an entrepreneur is the innocent optimism that they are going to be successful.'

'When you're young, you have no fear,' says Darpan. An entrepreneur does not start by thinking he's going to fail. According to Darpan, that self-belief is probably one of the most important qualities for an entrepreneur, and you need it to keep going.

His third venture was in the salon and spa domain, which led to the first avatar of MyGlamm five years later. Darpan was already running physical spas, and the MyGlamm wing started as an at-home spa service. That didn't really work, so his team pivoted and turned it into the MyGlamm make-up company, which further evolved into the Good Glamm Group, as we know it today.

'The most powerful weapon entrepreneurs have is self-belief.'

Darpan's journey from the age of nineteen, when he started his first venture, to age forty-two, when his start-up became a unicorn, is full of failures and learnings, which makes it truly inspirational. That he did not allow fear of failure to seep into his mind and always knew he would do something big is a shining example of remarkable self-belief.

'If I was not in the game, if I had given up at twenty-seven, if I had given up at thirty, if I had given up at thirty-five, if I had given up at thirty-seven—all the times when we pivoted—we would not have seen what we are seeing today.'

The biggest lesson Darpan has learned about entrepreneurship is that you have to keep finding ways to stay in the game. If you stay in the game long enough, your tipping point will eventually come. When it will come is a bit of a matter of destiny and differs from person to person, but it will definitely come.

Back in 2008, there were not many brands in India, especially in the beauty and wellness sector, so when Darpan came back to the country he decided to bring some brands to India. Darpan says, at that point in time, he did not have the courage to start a new brand, so what he did was to look for brands that he could bring to India.

The brand he went for was L'OCCITANE. Typically, when you go to these brands for franchises, you tell them how much money you are going to pay them and how many stores you are planning to open. But Darpan did not have the money to make any such offer. So, what could he do? He asked the brand to believe in him and promised them that the best L'OCCITANE spas would be in India.

It took him a year to convince them. Thankfully, the CEO of L'OCCITANE, André J. Hoffmann, is a very entrepreneurial man himself and took a bet on Darpan, and Darpan's one year of perseverance finally bore fruit.

From the age of thirty to thirty-five, Darpan brought twenty-five salons and spas to India. He understood beauty services, so in early 2015, when India was going through a tech boom, he decided to build MyGlamm, the at-home salon service business.

The problem was that when Darpan got the idea for the business India was seeing an investment boom, but by the time he launched the business an investment winter had set in and went on till the end of 2016. None of the VCs Darpan contacted were signing any cheques at the time. So, he once again contacted the CEO of L'OCCITANE and asked him if he would be interested in investing $1 million in a business he was starting.

Since Darpan had delivered on the promises he had made at the time of launching the salon business, André was happy to join him and wired him $2 million the next day. And that is how Darpan was able to keep his company afloat.

'The challenges and the pivots keep happening, what's important is to keep learning from them.'

Six months later, Darpan and his team had run out of money again as they were not able to solve the challenge of disintermediation, that is, reducing the number of intermediaries between producers and consumers. So, Darpan went to André and told him that the business was not working and he wanted to pivot to a D2C beauty brand. André agreed to invest, and that is how the MyGlamm make-up brand as you see it today was born.

Darpan still remembers vividly how excited they were when they received the first ten, twenty-five and fifty orders. They had a celebration when they hit 100 orders. Today, MyGlamm caters to 1.5 million orders every month.

MyGlamm chose different marketing tactics to promote its products. Darpan recalls that once they put a MyGlamm make-up at a ladies' kitty party, and everyone there just went crazy stall over the packaging, formulations and everything else. This was before they launched in stores like Lifestyle and Shopper's Stop, so it was a nice validation as well.

Darpan believes that in order to build a great brand there are two requirements—innovative products and disruptive marketing. When they were launching their lipstick, they roped in actor Siddharth Malhotra and put lipstick marks all over him. They posted a photo of this with the line, 'Tested on Sid, not tested on animals'. And the campaign went viral.

When they were launching their HD make-up, they on-boarded actor Sonakshi Sinha and did a fake news campaign. A picture of her getting arrested went viral on the Internet, and everyone was asking why she was arrested. The next day a picture of the actor was posted with the line, 'I got arrested for looking so damn good'. This campaign too became a huge success.

A lot of their marketing in their initial days was very unusual and very disruptive. That DNA of being disruptive continues to this day as they sponsor shows like Koffee with Karan and Bigg Boss with very unique brand positioning.

'The part of staying in the game comes later, at first you need to start the game.'

If you don't have a co-founder, it doesn't mean you will wait and look for one. As an entrepreneur you should go ahead and do what you need to do; you'll eventually find your co-founder. Some people are scared to take the plunge on their own, but Darpan advises that one should just do it and not overthink it. Once you have done that, do whatever you can to survive. As you survive, you'll keep learning and keep getting better at what you are doing. If you find a natural fit with the co-founder, go for a partnership as that can add a lot of value, but don't wait for that to happen. Take the plunge, and you'll figure it all out.

If you are in a job and dreaming of starting up, your job becomes your golden handcuff. It becomes especially hard if you have a family to look after. So, before you think of taking the plunge, see that you have enough funds to survive for at least two years. You will have to assume that for the next two years, you won't be making any money. It is only when you have that financial aspect sorted out that you can think of taking the plunge.

'The fire in a person is more important than the skill set.'

After taking the plunge, the most important thing is to find the right set of people. In the initial days, it is very important to find people who have that fire in them. When you are starting up, everything that can go wrong will probably go wrong, so you need people who have the determination to power your venture along with you.

It also depends on the stage of hiring. Till, say, the first hundred people, you need fire. But after that stage, you need people who have a strong learning curve behind them. You need to find the right balance between experience and culture.

'Move quickly, decide quickly, learn fast, fail faster but never stop.'

When it comes to the culture at the Good Glamm Group, Darpan believes it is the ability to think audacious and move very quickly. When they see a trend, the thought isn't about how to make that one thing happen, instead it's about how to multiply it and make it a ten. If they were not audacious, they would not be where they are today. And Darpan hopes that what they are today is just a sliver of what they are going to be tomorrow.

'At the "Good" Glamm Group, they have a fundamental belief that if you want to be a great company, you have to do good.'

Darpan believes that work-life balance is very important. You cannot expect everyone to be always on, always running a hundred miles an hour, seven days a week, twenty-four hours a day, thirty days a month. That is not possible. Burnout happens. So, create a culture where everyone loves what they're doing and they have a commitment towards you, but you also have a commitment towards them. You should understand and appreciate that people have their own lives to lead, and if you want to build a successful and sustainable company you need to promote work-life balance.

'Never chase valuation, chase dilution.'

The Good Glamm Group has raised funds from some very prominent VCs like Prosus Ventures, Warburg Pincus, etc. When it comes to fundraising, Darpan warns that you should never run behind valuation, instead, you should chase dilution. Valuations change, but what you dilute is never going to come back.

Consider how much money you really need, as different businesses have different capital requirements. If you are in a business where you can bootstrap without much capital, then you don't need to raise huge funds. But if it's a business where capital can make a disproportionate impact on the value you create, then go for the capital.

You should be very particular about which partner from the venture capital fund will work with you, because just like your co-founder, this person will also have a huge impact on your journey. Darpan has seen a lot of good entrepreneurs struggle because they had investors they did not get along with. While which fund invests in you is important, which partner from the fund is going to work with you is much more important, he says.

You should give your investors the bad news as much as you can and be very open about it. As soon as you do that, they will start trusting you. The minute that trust is formed, you can truly start working as partners.

'Don't swim against the current, swim with it.'

Darpan advises being mindful of momentum and knowing which direction the current is flowing in. If you are in a period when funds are pouring in, go for crazy growth, ride the momentum, and you will reap the benefits. But if there is a funding winter, then you should be very mindful about your capital and conserve it. You should be very cognizant of what the macro-environment is and adapt to it.

'Pitch with complete clarity and don't stop pitching.'

One interesting thing about Good Glamm Group's cap table is that most of their investors had previously said no to them. One of their investors, Accel, had said no to them in 2015, then again in 2019, and yet again in 2020, finally coming on board in 2021. And that goes on to show Darpan's dedication.

Although a lot of investors had said no to him, Darpan still kept sending them the group's quarterly reports, and they joined a couple of years later as they saw progress.

Investors love it when they know entrepreneurs have complete clarity as to what they are building, what their differentiator is and what every other aspect of their business is. One thing to keep in mind while pitching is that a lot of investors will say no, in fact maybe ninety-nine out of hundred will say no, but you just need that one investor to say yes to turn the situation around.

When it comes to validating your ideas, Darpan believes that the only way to do it is by making them happen. You must go to your friends and family, test your ideas out and go with what your intuition is telling you. At the start of the journey, an entrepreneur's intuition is their biggest motivator. If you see some signs of validation, jump into executing your idea.

Talking about the vision of the company, Darpan says that they are building a digital beauty and personal care conglomerate, powered by content and creators. They are bringing different channels of content and mixing them with commerce. As a company, they just want to keep building and keep growing as the biggest player in the content-to-commerce industry. And for that, they have some of the biggest market players in different segments under their wing, like ScoopWhoop, POPxo, MissMalini, Vidooly, BabyChakra, etc.

When we asked Darpan what was the one question he would have liked to ask himself, had he been in our shoes, his answer really brought out his personality: 'What makes you not stop?' And we think he has already answered that by sharing his entire journey with us.

If there is one thing we learn from his journey, it is that no matter what happened, he never really stopped, and kept at it. As he rightly said:

'The only way to do something is by doing it.'

10

Groww

Start-up Name	Groww
Headquarters	Bengaluru, Karnataka, India
Sector	Financial Services, DIY Investing, Mutual Funds
Founders	Lalit Keshre, Harsh Jain, Neeraj Singh and Ishan Bansal
Founded	2016
Valuation	$3 billion (November 2021)
Website	www.groww.com

About Groww

Groww is a web-based investment platform that allows users to invest in mutual funds and equities directly. The company is a creator of a mutual fund direct access platform. Groww's technology is aimed to make investing simple, accessible, transparent, and fully paperless, allowing customers to invest in mutual funds without any difficulties.

—StartupTalky

The year 2020 saw a boom in the investment industry; more than Covid, it was the ease of investment that it could be rightly attributed to. A decade back, there was a lack of information, sure, but for the common people investing itself was a tiresome procedure. Thanks to the Internet, this task is getting easier. And one such company that is paving the way for ease of investment is Groww.

Even for Ishan Sharma, the first investment he made was through Groww, and that is thanks to their easy-to-use UI.

Groww is a company built by the Flipkart mafia—Lalit Keshre, Harsh Jain, Neeraj Singh, and Ishan Bansal. Lalit might be one of the Flipkart mafia, but that is not where his journey started. He comes from a middle-class family and had a very modest upbringing. Nearly one in three Indians comes from a middle-class family, so as inspiring as his story is, his journey will be as relatable too to most of us.

Education is a big deal in middle-class families. Our parents, grandparents and everyone close to us make huge sacrifices just so that we could have a good education. Lalit spent his childhood with his nana-nani because his village could not provide quality education. He went to the first and only English-medium school in his grandparents' village, so in some ways he was luckier than most of the others from his village.

Things changed when he went to IIT, of course. It was a huge cultural shift for him. He was not the best person there; so many there were so much better than he was at so many things. At IIT, he saw a MacBook for the first time, and that was a very fascinating experience for him. This made him realize how much more there was for him to see and learn, and gave him the zeal to learn and become better at whatever he did.

He learnt to learn at IIT. There were so many good people there, so many things to do and so much to learn. IIT taught him to be a learning machine.

For Lalit, the idea of starting a business has always been about finding the solution to a problem that he himself faced. To solve such a problem was why he began his first start-up after college, Eduflix. Coming from a small town, he was nervous when he studied for the IIT JEE tests, and that was the problem he tried solving with Eduflix.

Solving a difficulty that you directly face and over which you can empathize with others who face it is a good way to solve a consumer problem. And if you are trying to solve a consumer problem that millions of others like you face, you can really scale that business.

What did not work for Eduflix was the fact that it was probably ahead of its time. Back in 2011, Jio did not exist and the Internet wasn't as accessible as it is today. And although Eduflix was solving a consumer problem, a company whose business model is based on video streaming wasn't really scalable at that time. So, that start-up failed and Lalit joined Flipkart, but he knew he would eventually be launching another start-up.

For Lalit, going to Flipkart was like going back to IIT. People around him were smart, and he was learning new things every day about customer obsession and scaling. Overall, it was a very meaningful experience. But from the very beginning, he was clear that he would be starting again, and then it was all about finding a new business opportunity.

When you come across a new opportunity, you have the advantage of looking at it from a beginner's point of view. You need to look at the problems customers are facing. Imagine that you are a person who does not know much about investing; you do not know what process to follow and your agent is not giving you all the information you need. What would be your thought process? As a financial services company, you need to tap into that thought process and try to solve the problems it contains with a scalable business model.

'When you come across a new opportunity, you have the advantage of looking at it from a beginner's point of view.'

Groww's consumer-first approach can clearly be seen in its YouTube channel. A financial services company does not need to have a free resource for customers where they can learn about investing. But Groww does. Lalit believes that when you are eliminating the middleman or agent, you need to give people tools with which to learn on their own. This helps them to access the service you are providing.

He had found a viable business; the next thing was to find the right co-founders. Luckily for him, he did not have to go further than Flipkart.

Lalit Keshre, Harsh Jain, Neeraj Singh and Ishan Bansal all worked at Flipkart. But how did Lalit choose his co-founders? What was the thing he looked for in his partners? Well, for him, more than complementary skills, the partners needed to have matching philosophies. There should not be a mismatch between the impact you and your co-founders want to make in this world. The most important thing for the Groww founders is customer obsession—they never want to compromise on customer trust and on this front, their values had to match. So, if you share matching values and philosophies in life, you have found your perfect co-founders.

Now, how do you find your co-founders? You look for people you know really, really well and have worked with. You might have studied with them; you might have worked with them or they might be your relative, but knowing people well is the key to finding your co-founder.

After you have your co-founders, you need to find your founding team. Ownership, value alignment, customer obsession and hunger to learn new things are some of the features that you will find in the Groww team. Lalit believes that if as a founder you're spending most of your time managing people, then it will become very hard for you to grow your start-up. And that is why it is very important to have a founding team that believes in ownership and shares the same values as you.

When you take the plunge of leaving your job and starting your own venture, just as the Groww founders did, there enters the unavoidable fear of failure. So, how do you tackle that? Lalit believes that if somebody is saying they do not fear failure, they are probably lying. There is always a fear of failure. How you deal with that fear is what matters. For Lalit, the important question to ask is why you fear failure, and then try to answer that question. We are human beings, and trying to justify emotional problems with logical answers is hard. But when you note down what you fear and why, it becomes easier for you to tackle it. You need to have continuous conversations with yourself in order to cope with that fear of failure.

Now you have a viable business, co-founders and a great founding team. What next? How do you acquire customers and reduce customer acquisition costs (CAC)? According to Lalit, the first set of users always consists of your family and friends. One interesting thing about Groww is that most of their customers are from a middle-class background. That is because most of the founding team is from that segment. The people who initially started using Groww referred them to others, and so on. Through word-of-mouth publicity, Groww was able to acquire its customers. If you want to reduce CAC, you need to enable word-of-mouth recommendation, and that only happens when you have a good product to offer.

Although Groww has nearly 3 million subscribers on YouTube, an unprecedented milestone for most companies, Lalit does not see it as a customer acquisition channel. Since Groww is a platform where people have to do everything on their own, they need to give customers a mode by which to learn so that they can make sensible financial decisions for themselves.

It also serves as a great mode for Lalit to understand what his customers think about the business. He loves going through comments and emails. The worst thing you can find in a customer, he believes, is indifference to your product. But if they hate it or love it, it shows that they care about it.

After all of this, it all comes down to raising funds for your start-up. Groww has some of the best VCs in the world, like Tiger Global and Sequoia Capital India. Satya Nadella is also an independent investor and advisor in Groww. In fact, it is the only Indian company he has invested in. So, how did it raise money? For Lalit, the right way of thinking is not to aim for 'raising money' but to think about how much of the company you are going to sell. Instead of thinking 'Oh! I raised 10 million', think about it, like, 'I sold 10 per cent of the company'. If you think you can sustain without selling a part of your company, then why raise funds at all? When you change your way of thinking, you can better realize the worth of your equity.

If you understand VCs well, it will be easier for you to raise money. You need to present them with what they are looking for. Now, that does not mean you need to change your business model—that is the biggest mistake you can make as an entrepreneur. You need to understand that some businesses are not VC businesses, and that is completely okay.

So, what is the most valuable skill you will look for if you want to build a start-up? For Lalit it is curiosity. Some people are naturally curious, but reading plays a very important part as well in growing this curiosity. People need to ask questions and not accept things at face value. For a budding entrepreneur, it is of monumental importance to be curious.

Suppose you launched a start-up and were able to make it a billion-dollar entity, what do you do with the money? Some people love to spend it on luxuries, but not Lalit. Coming from a modest background, money meant freedom for him. Freedom to do what he wants. He believes that when you have money you have control over how you utilize your time. You can use it to show off to people that you are wealthy or you can use it to have control over your time and happiness—the choice is yours.

When it comes to upcoming businesses, he is most excited about, they are always consumer-driven. Whether it is financial services, education or anything related to the Internet, if a business is consumer-driven, Lalit would be interested in it.

To evaluate whether your business idea is good or not, ask yourself what drives you. If you work on solving a problem that you and millions of others like you have faced, you might be able to create a successful business.

The one question Lalit would have liked to ask himself was: 'If you're doing something, what are the reasons that you shouldn't do it?' He believes that this is a crucial question, the answer to which will help you to get the complete picture of what you are embarking upon. Once you have both the pros and cons about your business idea, you can evaluate whether it will become a viable business and whether you can *groww* or not.

II

Mamaearth

Start-up Name	Mamaearth
Headquarters	Gurugram, Haryana, India
Sector	Personal care products
Founders	Ghazal Alagh and Varun Alagh
Founded	2016
Valuation	$2 billion (December 2022)
Website	www.mamaearth.in

About Mamaearth

Mamaearth is a D2C brand that comes under the umbrella of Honasa Consumer Limited, which is the largest digital-first BPC company in India. It sells baby and personal care products. It was launched in 2016 by the husband-wife pair Varun Alagh and Ghazal Alagh.

'Jack of all, master of none . . . is still better than the master of one.'

Ghazal was one of those kids in school who are good at almost everything. She was considered to be the artist of her school and her paintings were appreciated by everyone around. She was equally good in maths and science too. Everyone told her to choose science as it was considered the natural path to success. And so she did.

But that distanced her from art and she stopped painting altogether. It wasn't until she got married and moved to the Philippines that she picked up the paintbrush again. But still, she didn't think of selling any of her pieces because she felt buyers would be biased against her as she was not a professionally trained artist and was hence not qualified to sell her works.

It wasn't until she moved to New York and got a degree in Art that she started exhibiting her paintings. And, to her surprise, she sold some twenty-five to thirty paintings at a really good price. It was a big encouragement for her.

When Varun and Ghazal were expecting their first child, they found a lack of good quality, toxin-free baby products in the market. They started importing products from the US, but that was a costly affair. They realized it was not just they who were facing this problem; there were hundreds of other parents who were in the same boat. They wanted to create safer alternatives for baby products in India, and hence Mamaearth was born.

'If you have a bigger dream and feel that your idea is solving a problem that you are really passionate about, then don't let anything make you believe otherwise.'

If she had nursed the same mindset she had about not being able to sell her paintings, she wouldn't have been able to start Mamaearth either, because she was hardly qualified when it came to baby products. But the purpose behind starting Mamaearth was so strong that she decided that no matter what happened, she would figure it out. And so she did.

'Indian consumers are not "price conscious", they are "value conscious."'

Many people think that Indian consumers are price conscious, but Varun thinks they're value conscious. That's the discovery they have made with Mamaearth. If you are able to demonstrate the value that you are delivering to them, Indian consumers are willing to pay a premium for it.

The other thing they learnt about consumers was how quickly they adopted technology. If something is making their lives convenient, people are willing to adopt it very quickly. For example, if people can get stuff delivered to their homes at better prices compared to what is available in the market, they'll switch easily—it's a no-brainer.

Mamaearth raised $500,000 from Fireside Ventures in the very first round of funding. Then came Stellaris Venture Partners, and when they were at the Rs 100-crore run rate, then came Sequoia. So, who could be better to guide through the world of VCs than Varun and Ghazal Alagh?

'Whether you need money or not depends on the objective of your business.'

According to Varun, you should know your business objective and why you are raising funds. The objective could be growth, acquisition, or something else, but it most definitely cannot be that someone else has raised money so you need to too.

Some founders tend to dilute a large chunk of their business at the beginning itself, and that's the reason why a lot of them have substantially lower ownership when their businesses actually become big and meaningful.

Varun says, 'A lot of people raise significantly more than required during the idea or product-market fit stages, and that hurts massively later on.' He advises founders to understand how much money they require to help their business reach the next level of its evolution, as that helps in avoiding early dilution of the business.

'You should get the right-sized investor at the right time.'

Varun believes there is an ideal set of investors for every size of business. Founders tend to go for bigger brand names in the initial stages, but that isn't helpful, in his opinion. The main problem with trying to get a bigger name initially is that it's far more difficult. What you really need at that stage are angel investors, as they are more driven and can provide you with the mentorship you need to solve your problems. They also help in connecting you to the next set of investors, who tend to be early-stage investors.

The early-stage investors need to spend a lot of time on the company, work along with the founders, help them find connections and hustle with them to build the business, so their cheque size tends to be smaller, but that's what the business needs at that point in time.

'It's in the interest of angel investors to get early-stage investors for the business, and for them to get the next set of investors, and so on, which creates a beautiful chain.'

As a founder, you shouldn't try to overreach. You can get the bigger names, but their organization and their DNA are not designed to support you at that stage. Their interests won't be aligned with yours as your value will be a very small drop in their fund, so it wouldn't really matter to them much, which you will regret later.

'Marriage is the most important decision in life, finding a co-founder is a close second.'

Finding a co-founder for your start-up is hard, but thankfully Varun didn't have to go further than home.

Since Varun and Ghazal were facing the problem together, there wasn't really anyone better for Varun to start this venture with. It was a natural choice. But looking objectively at it, Varun believes the most important thing you should look for in a co-founder is trust.

'There is no Tinder for co-founders.'

You are going to invest a significant amount of time into building your start-up, so if you can't trust the people who are building it with you, you will always be watching your back and you will not be able to build it. In Varun and Ghazal's case, they have spent five years together, so the level of trust was already there.

You need to ask yourself, do I trust this person emotionally? How do I feel around him or her? Are we vulnerable with each other? Are we comfortable telling honest truths to each other? These questions will really help you in finding your co-founders.

The second thing you need to look for in your co-founders is complementary skills. You don't want to be replicas of each other. Apart from capabilities, your temperaments should complement too. If you are an aggressive person, having a co-founder who is calm and patient really helps.

'You have to bring the right people to run the business with you.'

Like every other founder, Varun also spent almost half of his time hiring the initial set of people, and he believes there is no other way to build a great business. From a trade perspective, there are few things that they valued a little more than traditional industries do. They valued hunger far more than experience. They valued learning agility and how quickly a person scales more than what a person already knows or what degrees they hold.

Ghazal believes that what kind of people you hire depends on which phase of hiring you are in. When you are hiring the first ten people for your business, you need to look for hustlers, people who can figure things out and get them done. Ghazal herself learnt a lot of things from

Googling, researching and talking to the right set of people. So she believes others can too.

> **'Then we needed people who were better than us, who knew more than us and who could add much more value compared to the way we were thinking.'**

When you're in the phase of hiring the next ten to hundred people, Ghazal believes you need to look for domain experts. Be it content, growth, strategy or marketing, you need to have people who can get the stuff done in their respective areas.

And then when they got bigger, Ghazal wanted Mamaearth to be a well-governed organization in terms of checks and standards, legalities, etc. So, when they hired the next 1,000 people, they looked for those who had relevant experience in the industry and hence could put the processes in place and also have the capability to build their own teams. One of the qualities she looked for was the leaders' comfort level in hiring people who were smarter than them, as that makes a huge difference.

> **'How the organization makes their employees feel is what defines the culture of the company.'**

For Varun, work culture is not about the food you serve in your canteens or the bean bags you have in your office. It is about how you and your organization take day-to-day decisions, how your people behave with each other, how they behave with the outside world, how they communicate with each other and how they feel as a part of the organization.

And hence, at Mamaearth, they have adopted a model of rituals, symbols, stories and heroes. Varun believes that these are the four things that can help create your organizational culture. How you ensure that all of these are designed to reward the right behaviours on a day-to-day basis differentiates your culture from others.

Mamaearth is an innovative organization that loves to experiment. And since people spend half of their lives at work, the team here believes in having fun while at it. There are no restrictions attached to the hierarchy here—anyone can ask any question or give suggestions. All of these things together define Mamaearth's culture.

In the long term, Varun wants Mamaearth to be the number one choice of Indian consumers in the beauty and personal care space. He wants it to become part of the day-to-day conversations of people for decades to come and a company which lasts for a hundred years.

'Kuch paane ke liye kuch khona padta hai.'
[To win something, you need to lose something.]

Varun didn't have time to meet his relatives and friends for the initial four or five years of setting up and running Mamaearth, as he and his team were so immensely engrossed in it. Varun believes that when you are building something, you start from zero. You need to understand that you had built an identity by working for years, but now that you're starting from scratch, you need to let go of that identity. If you do not, your attitude might stop you from achieving certain things, and then you will not be able to create as big a business as you want. Letting go of your previous identity is also a sacrifice.

Ghazal believes that work-life balance is a myth and you have to always keep a look at the larger picture. When she started Mamaearth, she was a new mother. Both her business and her baby needed equal time and attention. Raising both of these entities was so similar that it made it easier for her. However, on a lighter note, she mentions that raising a baby is more difficult than raising capital for the business.

What is the next step that will grow the business versus what to do with the baby for him to grow healthy? Both these were very similar concerns for Ghazal, and hence she found synergy in her twin roles as mother and entrepreneur.

The fact that Ghazal and Varun were both business as well as life partners worked in their favour. They had decided that whenever a situation arose where one had to prioritize either work or personal life, Ghazal would be the one prioritizing their son Agastya and Varun—the one prioritizing meetings and work.

The one question we asked every founder at the end of the interview was what would be the one question they would have asked themselves. For Varun, it would have been, 'What would you prioritize and in what order in the early stage of your start-up—people, product, capital or business model?'

The most limited resource you have in the beginning is your own bandwidth and focus, so where you spend them has a huge impact on how your business is going to scale. Do you spend it on perfecting your product or on raising capital or on hiring or on thinking about a business model? And, if you had to prioritize A versus B, what should it be? These questions make a huge difference, because they are strategic calls, and strategies are all about what you say no to rather than what you say yes to. The answer to these questions can help an early-stage founder in determining some of those priorities.

For Ghazal, that question would be whether she would prioritize fame or peace of mind. Since Ghazal has been a judge on the first season of the TV reality show Shark Tank India and has tasted her own share of fame, she says she'll always choose peace of mind. When it comes to fame, even if 90 per cent of it is good and only 10 per cent bad, that 10 per cent still starts affecting you. And she would always choose peace of mind over everything else.

'Product followed by people, these two are non-negotiables.'

For Ghazal, the product is the priority. The first experience a consumer has with your brand is through your product, and if that's sub-par, you lose the game right there. So, for her, the product is the first priority, followed by people. And when you have smart people on your team, they figure out how to bring in the capital and make things work.

'Mothers trust other mothers more than they do doctors, Google or anybody or anything else.'

And that's the philosophy they opted for Mamaearth. When they were only a baby care products brand, it was 'mothers trust mothers'. When they expanded and launched other categories, it was 'millennials trust millennials', and so on. It was the word of mouth that helped Mamaearth grow.

In the beginning, Ghazal identified some mothers who had a substantial following of mothers on social media and were part of parenting groups on Facebook. She connected with them for pure knowledge sharing and understanding as they were Mamaearth's target group. It helped in getting the word out there. And, as the influencer marketing industry grew, things fell into place and the company also grew.

It was a very honest approach of just sharing information, getting valuable feedback to help make a better product, and pitching better to the consumer so they could create content that people actually understood so that it became easier for those people to explain it further to others.

For the first four or five months of its creation, the Mamaearth website was purely for educational purposes. The founders knew they could sell through other mediums, but they wanted to educate people about what toxins were, what ingredients they were using, how their products were better than anyone else's in the market, what standards they were following to make their products safer, etc.

'Burning and scaling are fine but not sustainable.'

Coming from a business family, Ghazal knew that the only way to be in business is by earning profits. Although they were burning in order to scale, they were always on the lookout for when they saw themselves getting profitable, and that's what helped them achieve profitability much faster.

'Fear of failure is real.'

When you are starting to build something, the fear of failure is bound to seep in. It's very easy to talk about it and say something which is very motivational. One line Ghazal truly believes in is, 'The regret of not doing something that you really believed you should have tried is much more painful than the pain of failure.' And this helps her keep moving forward. In fact, we were amazed at her attitude of groundedness, even after having achieved so much in her life. While leaving from their office, she asked us if we would want a lift to go back to our hotel or not!

There will be many a self-doubt, but you'll eventually figure it out. Ghazal advises all aspiring entrepreneurs not to let their internal biases stop them from doing what they really want to achieve.

'You can live with failure, but you cannot live with regrets!'

12

OfBusiness

Start-up Name	OfBusiness
Headquarters	Gurugram, Haryana, India
Sector	Fintech, NBFC, Lending
Founders	Asish Mohapatra, Ruchi Kalra, Bhuvan Gupta, Nitin Jain and Vasant Sridhar
Founded	2015
Valuation	$5 billion (July 2022)
Website	www.ofbusiness.com

About OfBusiness

OFB Tech (OfBusiness) is a tech-enabled platform that enables SMEs in the infrastructure and industrial sectors to acquire raw materials and obtain finance. It incorporates technology into SME purchasing

behaviour to provide clients with better items, at better costs, and in shorter time frames, as well as with extensive online and offline assistance.
— Start-up Talky

'Money is the currency of life.'

If you want to make it big in life, you need to make money. The best way to make money is by doing some business. This thought was instilled very early on in Asish Mohapatra's life. His parents were doing PhD at IIT Kharagpur, so his early childhood days were spent there. He experienced a cultural shift when he moved from IIT Kharagpur to Cuttack in Odisha, a city with a small-town atmosphere. This shift, in some ways, marked the onset of his entrepreneurial journey.

Growing up in a turbulent environment like IIT Kharagpur where everyone was always discussing some high-end ideas to moving to a sleepy locality in Odisha where nobody really cares about anything was a life-altering experience for Asish Mohapatra.

The difference could be seen in how the people talked and what they talked about. In Kharagpur, it had all been about books, science and creating something; in Cuttack, people talked about getting a job at an MNC, becoming a software engineer or joining their father's business. When you get to experience such drastically different environments, you realize what you want for your own life. And Asish wanted the former environment.

It's safe to say the seed of entrepreneurship, the thought that you have to do something in life, was planted very early on in Asish. But what does a ten-year-old know about making a difference? All he knew was he had to become famous. But again, how does one become famous? That was a question Asish started asking the people around him. Someone told him that to become famous you needed to be good at some form of art.

That was where the journey of trying things out began. He tried writing, singing, mimicry . . . and at one point had eighteen to nineteen hobbies, all born out of one and one wish only—to stand out and become famous.

While dabbling in many activities, the realization struck that to make it big in life it is not enough to be just good at something, you have to make money too. And to make money, you have to be good at business too.

As a kid, the best way to have some money is by asking your parents for it, but that's taking money, not making money.

Once again Asish dabbled in many things to make money. When he was in High School, he sold micro-investments, started trading in commodities, even selling coal. And that was his introduction to business.

People began to ask questions—How much money was he making? Was he doing something illegal? How much was he saving? What would happen to his business while he was at school? Although he did not realize it at the time, these were some valuable business lessons.

The first lesson was about growth—you have to make more money than you made in the previous month. The next was about compliance—to run a successful business, you can't do something illegal. Then it was about making profits—it's not enough to make money, you have to save some too. And then the most important one was on team building—you need your business to go on even when you are not present.

These are big business words now, but while growing up, the concepts they represent were part of Asish's life.

Business is all fun and games, but when you are being brought up in an academic household, you need to focus on your studies too. Asish's mother was a professor, and his father a scientist, so his inclination towards academics was almost natural.

'The entire world was moving towards technology and I realized I was not there.'

He went to IIT, did his Engineering, worked at ITC, went for an MBA, worked at McKinsey and then at Matrix. He was from an old-world economy and the world was moving towards technology. It was very apparent to him as a VC at Matrix that unless he dabbled in technology, he would not be able to become a good VC. And that was when the entrepreneurship *keeda* kicked back in. After all, if you have to learn and start something new, why not do it for yourself instead of doing it for someone else?

'Master the art of selling.'

Before trying to be good at sales, you need to understand why you are selling. The objective of a sale should always be to make the other person give away something—it could be money, business, or something else.

Now, there are two components to sales—first you have to WOW the other person, and then you have to negotiate.

You have to understand what you are really good at and then use that to wow the person. One method of wowing could be by being a great storyteller. You could connect a lot of dots and make the whole world look like a very compact and interrelated place. Or you can use logic. The third way could be through your persona and by being a good talker. You can pick whatever method fits you best and whatever weapon of choice, but the objective should be just one—to wow the guy you are selling to.

Once you have impressed your potential buyer, that person would be happy to spend time with you and hear what you have to say. Now that you have their attention, you can get into negotiations. One thing to keep in mind is that negotiation always comes from a place of authority— you cannot negotiate by sucking up; you need to have the upper hand.

Negotiation itself involves many tactics. You can influence someone, manipulate them, put pressure on them or use logic. You have to pick whatever method fits best for you.

A good salesman will always wow the other person first and then get on to sell; a bad salesman tends to do the opposite. Be a good salesman.

'In the initial stages, your start-up is who you are. Later it becomes what people want.'

You have to look at what industry you are good at, understand the problems in that area and provide a solution. Asish was a kickass sales guy. He had sold to a lot of SMEs when he was a kid; he had run an SME while at

ITC and he had invested in a few SMEs as well. So, doing something around SMEs made sense to him. At the same time in the 2010s, a lot of action started happening in the SME and B2B space, a lot of good talent that he would have liked to work with was joining this space, and a lot of capital was being invested there as well.

So, for Asish the logical choice was to go for something related to SMEs because that was what he had always done in his life; the people whom he would want to work with were there, and that was where the money was too.

Now that he had identified the industry and what he was good at, he had to figure out the problems of that industry. The major problem he noticed was that most of the SMEs did not know the price of the materials they were buying. Since he had previously sold coal, working as a middleman, he knew that there were good margins there. These were all commerce-related problems.

He realized that there was a working capital problem too in the SME space and that the middleman doubled up as a financier as well as a commerce provider. Now the question was, should he pick finance or should he pick commerce?

Around the same time, Asish met his future partner, both in business and in life. Ruchi was a finance person, and together they thought, why not take the bull by both horns? He could handle commerce and Ruchi finance, so why not do both? And that was how OfBusiness was born.

You have your billion-dollar idea, now what? Now you need to find yourself one or more partners. But what do you need to look for in a partner? For Asish, it was easy to decide. He had had a lot of co-founders since he was a kid and had made a lot of mistakes, so now he had a formula. And that, too, a really good one!

Asish likes to go for people who are hands-on—not people who get the stuff done but the ones who do the stuff. For, when you are hands-on you know the ground reality, you pick up data from the ground yourself. Next, Asish likes good leaders—people who don't just know things but are also willing to teach others those things. Third, Ashish likes people who really slog it out. These are the three very important traits Asish wants in the people who will partner with him.

Apart from the qualities discussed above, your co-founder should possess something that you do not have or do not aspire to have. They should have two abilities that completely differentiate them from you. When someone possesses something you don't, you have an inherent respect for them.

'Three sets of common values plus two differentiators.'

As long as a person has these attributes, they can be a partner. Now, whether they can be a co-founder depends on the stage they are at in their own journey of life. OfBusiness started with six co-founders because they all were at the same stage of their journeys at the same time.

'The secret sauce: It's not the strategy that matters but the execution.'

'Fundamentally, I don't believe that there should be any strategy that can differentiate you from others,' says Asish. The strategy the founders chose was to do commerce and finance together. Some ventures were doing commerce only and some were focusing on finance alone, but there was nobody doing both, especially on an institutional scale. What OfBusiness did was pick both. The thing is, both businesses work independently, but the problem they faced was at the execution level, which they solved by investing in young talent.

They do not hire from the industry; they hire freshers, especially investing in them by teaching them what they know. The good thing with freshers is that they do not come with baggage and there is nothing for them to unlearn. They learn everything at the company. If you look at the OfBusiness team, all their geography and department heads were hired as freshers.

This strategy did not pay off initially as the freshers were still learning. But after a year or two, when it did pay off, it really paid off. OfBusiness's strategy was already very different, and all they needed was execution to make it.

The second way the founders solved their problem was by having extremely hands-on people in the very beginning. They had young talent who were ready to give their everything to the start-up, and that made execution easy.

Your strategy can be easily copied, but nobody can copy your execution—and that was what made OfBusiness different from the rest.

'We fail very fast; hence we fail very often.'

When you are running a start-up, you will face many challenges. Some of them you will be able to solve and some will result in failure. What you have to focus on is how much time you take to let go of something that is not working. You must try several things before you find what actually works for you. Once you realize what is working, put all your energy into it. And when you find something that is not working, shut it out in no time.

'The best way to learn is to learn from your own journey.'

Your journey gives you an insight into what works for you and what does not. What you do should be a mirror image of your own past. Talk to people, watch interviews, read books and listen to podcasts, but in the end, do what you have learned from your life and what has worked for you.

Building a start-up calls for hiring of people. You have to be very picky when it comes to the people you hire because they become instrumental in the success or failure of your start-up. At OfBusiness, they hire young talent. There are four crucial traits they look for in an employee— commercial instinct, hunger, not having had it easy in life and a flair for communication. Employees should understand the value of money, and they should have the hunger to achieve something in life. When you have not had it easy in life, you know the value of things and of ways to get things done. Most importantly, you should have a flair for communication. These traits don't just make for an ideal employee; they also make for successful people.

Coming to the company culture, OfBusiness follows ABC—altruism, brotherhood and camaraderie. Altruism means you want to do good things for others, brotherhood means doing things for others because it's your duty to, and camaraderie means you enjoy doing it. So, ABC essentially means doing good for others while feeling that it is your duty to do so but enjoying it at the same time.

RAJ in Hindi means to rule, but it also stands for Reliance, Adani and Bajaj. Every business has a vision, and OfBusiness's is RAJ. Reliance excels at manufacturing, supply chain and global imports; Adani thinks big and thinks fast; and Bajaj is all about understanding financing to the core and building it in a really, really profitable way. OfBusiness wants to be a combination of the three.

Before coming to what works, you should know what does not work. Most people end up doing their own basic market research. They first pitch their idea to the people they trust. Since these people want to avoid conflict in case they disagree, they may give their go-ahead to the idea even if they don't like it. Then the entrepreneurs go and ask the people they do not trust. Now, these people do not care enough for them or their ideas to give them a spare thought. And that is why doing either is a wrong approach.

If you have an idea, instead of going around and asking people what they think, you need to go ahead and just execute it. Put your time, money and energy into it, give it everything you have got. As long as you're putting in these three things, you will get the right answers.

But how do you know if your idea is big enough? You cannot know this unless other people come and join you. You cannot make it large yourself, you need people who believe in your idea. That is the start of a start-up.

Asish strongly believes in giving back to society, and the question he would have liked to ask himself is about that—

'How do you give back?' He was a VC for five years and has been an entrepreneur for almost seven. He is amongst the people who have seen the start-up ecosystem very closely. He says who he is today is because of the community he comes from, and so it is his responsibility to give back to that community. Well, Asish is one of the founders who literally connected us with almost everyone we wanted to. He asked us to share our list, and we shamelessly sent him an Excel sheet containing the list of founders we wanted to connect to. He was so kind as to create separate WhatsApp groups for us with each of them.

There are three ways one can give back. The simplest one is by investing in companies. The other is through philanthropic activities; but the most crucial way is by mentoring young entrepreneurs, who are just starting out in life. There is enough money in the country; what people really need is the experience of people who have already been through the process of creating a start-up. When you share your experience with one person, that person shares it with several others, and that's how a chain gets formed which keeps on going and growing.

'Money is available in abundance in India. What people really need is the experience of people who have been through starting up.'

13

Oxyzo

Start-up Name	Oxyzo
Headquarters	Gurugram, Haryana, India
Sector	Credit, Financial services
Founders	Ruchi Kalra, Asish Mohapatra, Bhuvan Gupta, Nitin Jain and Vasant Sridhar
Founded	April 2016
Valuation	$1 billion (March 2022)
Website	www.oxyzo.in

About Oxyzo

Oxyzo is the lending arm of OfBusiness. It is a non-banking finance company registered with the RBI and offers business-to-business credit facilities to small and medium enterprises. Oxyzo is currently serving 5000+ SMEs across India and has an AUM of Rs 3,000+ crore.

Only 15 per cent of Indian unicorns have women founders. But Ruchi Kalra is changing that number, one unicorn at a time. Of the only twenty-three profitable unicorns in India, Ruchi has sat at the helm of two of them. Starting as OfBusiness Group's financing platform, Oxyzo didn't just enter the unicorn club; it entered at the Series A level itself.

So, how did she do it? Was this always the plan? Not really, sometimes things do not work out as planned, but most of the time it is because there is something better in store for us.

Before we start the chapter, we want to tell you how humble Ruchi is. When we spoke to her on our call and asked her if she could connect us with someone from Oxyzo's PR team, she replied, *'We don't have any PR Team. You can directly co-ordinate with me about the timings and venue. We are also normal human beings.'* We were awestruck. When we reached Delhi on 3 June 2022, she herself greeted us at the reception and showed us around her office. She wanted to know more about why we were writing the book, and after a candid chat of fifteen minutes, we began our interview!

For Ruchi, the plan was simple—do an MBA, work as a consultant for two or three years, figure out which industry she liked best and get into that industry. But then she started working in the financial services segment at McKinsey, and she loved it so much that she did it for nine years!

'You never know what is in store for you, you just find your passion.'

Ruchi found it in the financial services industry. That was what she pursued at OfBusiness too. It was her love for financial services that eventually gave birth to Oxyzo. Was it easy? Given that she was doing what she loves to do and had been doing it for a while? Not really.

Ruchi believes that whether you start at twenty or thirty, there is never a substitute for hard work. And building OfBusiness and then Oxyzo had been nothing but hard work.

Apart from that, you need to find your intent too. Whether you are in school, college, or at work, you should know what your goal is. Once you know that, everything else starts to come together to make it happen.

'Instead of externalizing that I'm not able to do something because of X, Y and Z reasons, you should say, "I want to do this. What else can come together and help me achieve this?"'

For everything to come together, you need people who will help you in your endeavour. You cannot do everything on your own. You need a support system, you need a team. It's always a collective effort.

Where you come from has a lot of bearing on where you go. McKinsey was instrumental in instilling the values Ruchi cherishes and in teaching her the importance of hard work, intent and collective effort. In any good consulting firm, you learn to perform beyond your weight, identify issues and provide solutions, and that was what McKinsey did for Ruchi. This helped her discover herself, which in turn accelerated the path to discovering what she could do.

Consulting teaches you to be curious and inquisitive. You learn to go to the root cause of a problem, understand the ground operations and then come up with a solution. It also teaches you the 80-20 rule—which means you cannot solve all problems on your own. You need to figure out the core problem, the 20 per cent, which can give you 80 per cent results.

It is the same culture that Ruchi has tried to instil in her start-ups. At OfBusiness as well as Oxyzo, your age does not determine the work you do. At Oxyzo it's very important for everyone there to understand the importance of credit. Everyone is like family, and the entrepreneurial zeal in people is recognized and appreciated. There is no formal structure people have to follow; anyone can talk to anyone, and that has helped build a very strong culture within the organization.

Oxyzo is doing very well today, but how did it all start? When things are going great at the job you are doing, how do you decide to take the plunge? Well, there is never just one thing that can make you take some life-changing decision; more often than not it is a combination of two or three factors. Ruchi was at a stage in her life where she wanted to build something she could call her own. She had met Asish and Bhuvan, so she had the right set of people and an ecosystem in place too. But it was a bit more personal than that. There was this voice in her head that was telling her she needed a change of trajectory and that it was the right time. She listened to that voice and took the plunge.

Everything was changing in Ruchi's life. She took a break as she was expecting a baby and was moving from Mumbai to Delhi. She did not have any baggage and it felt like the right time for her to take the plunge. She, Asish and Bhuvan wanted to build something ground up that they could call their own. And, as she said in the beginning, when you really want something, everything comes together to help you achieve it. The right set of people, the timing and a supportive investor ecosystem encouraged them to take the plunge.

The most important thing is to make a decision and be ready for the repercussions, whether good or bad. You can't be scared. Fear is the last thing that should be on your mind.

'Entrepreneurship makes you feel great, but it's also a great responsibility.'

Ruchi and Asish left their jobs to start their entrepreneurial journey. Should you also do the same? According to Ruchi, you should not start something of your own just because you saw a Shark Tank episode or your friend is doing it or because you are bored. You can get enough entrepreneurial thrill from your job. If you have an idea, ask yourself if it is the right idea, one that can make money or turn into something big. Then find people who can help you achieve that goal.

A single person does not have all the skills required to run a venture, and hence you need a team. How do you find that team? First of all, you should be ready to share a piece of the pie with the people you decide to work with. And then you need to find people you respect and trust to come along and help turn your dream into a reality.

That is how Ruchi did it. Financial services was close to her heart and lending has always been a profitable business that will make money and grow and sustain itself, if done right. That was the genesis of Oxyzo.

As a platform in the B2B space, you cannot solve for commerce until you solve for credit. Ruchi saw an opportunity in this and thought: instead of doing it for a platform why not do it for the entire ecosystem? They did the commercials on it and it made sense from an ROE (return on equity) point of view, and that was how Oxyzo was born. Ruchi believes that if you have thought through what you want to do and if it is making commercial sense, then the only thing you need to focus on is execution.

OfBusiness has a team of five founders—Ruchi Kalra, Asish Mohapatra, Bhuvan Gupta, Nitin Jain and Vasant Sridhar—although Ruchi believes that in essence, they have an extended team of twenty. But there are five or six key people who helped in building Oxyzo. So, how did they hire them?

'If you hire As, people under them will be great and then they'll get great people under them. If the first layer that you hire is Bs, the Bs will always recruit a C and so on.'

Someone had once said these lines to Ruchi and they stuck with her ever since. People are the most important part of a business and you have to recruit right. But the responsibility of recruiting all 500 right people is not with the top four or five people. You just have to make sure the first layer of people is right. Because if the first layer itself consists of talented people, they will in turn hire talented people too.

One more thing to keep in mind while hiring people is to give them enough time to grow. The people you hire could be A, but when you give them enough time and responsibility to grow, they will turn into A. This is the reason why OfBusiness and Oxyzo have such great teams.

You have to be flexible with these people too. You cannot put them under the constraints of a nine-to-five job; you need to give them ownership of their work and the flexibility to get the work done on their terms.

'Apart from their respective duties, all the people in the team have a single common duty, and that's towards the company.'

The most important thing for Ruchi is trust. You should be able to assign different work to different people and trust that it will all get done without your interference. Apart from that, having a common vision for the team is very important.

Oxyzo had a great idea and an amazing team, but what worked out for them was that they were solving a core problem. They knew what their target segment was and what product they needed. The fact that they were not just providing funds but also a platform to buy raw materials from really worked for them.

'You cannot start up if you have a fear of failure.'

If you are building your start-up there is no place for fear of failure. Fear comes from your insecurities, and you end up asking whether you are good enough or not, or whether your co-founders are good enough or not. If you have a fear of failure you are doing a disservice to yourself, to your family and to the people who came along with you and the investors' money. If you have liabilities you should not get into entrepreneurship because your responsibilities lie someplace else. You can find a lot of entrepreneurial responsibilities at your workplace and you should go for that instead.

Oxyzo has been profitable since year one. For a business to grow it is very important to build trust. How did Oxyzo build trust? By showing return on capital. Oxyzo went through in five years' time the different cycles that a regular company goes through in twenty. They had to mature much faster. Their fundamental building blocks were correct and their customer retention was high. They knew what their metrics are and what they would translate into, and this helped them grow into a profitable business.

Ruchi wants Oxyzo to become a diversified digital financial services platform with multiple financial services businesses. She wants Oxyzo to be a company that other companies look up to and want to emulate.

Ruchi advises youngsters to read more. Knowing what is happening around the world has become more important than ever before as it has an effect on what is happening in the country. If you want to be good at your work you need to think beyond your job description. You also need to be a little bit more well-versed with other roles and other requirements of the company to be better at what you do.

The best ideas are those related to something you are passionate about and have the necessary skills for. Some problems are not meant to be solved. Your idea should solve a genuine problem that customers are also willing to pay for.

Does the day of an entrepreneur at Oxyzo look different from those of other people in the organization? Not really. Ruchi's day looks exactly the same as that of any other employee's at Oxyzo. She has some work that she needs to do, and she does it. She believes that if her day starts looking different from anyone else's in the team, she will be very disconnected from the organization.

Had she been in our shoes, Ruchi would have loved to ask herself: 'What keeps you excited and how is it different from your previous life?' Life changes, and you also change with it. Earlier in her life, Ruchi used to look a lot for external validation. But that is gone now.

Now it is about how the company is doing, about whether the people with her are happy or not, whether they growing or not. It becomes more about what you are building in terms of people and the organization and about how people are perceiving the organization than about yourself.

When you build a start-up, your focus changes from *I* to *us*.

14

OYO

Start-up Name	OYO
Headquarters	Gurugram, Haryana, India
Sector	Hospitality
Founder	Ritesh Agarwal
Founded	2012
Valuation	$6.5 billion (October 2022)
Website	oyorooms.com

About OYO

OYO is a global hospitality technology marketplace that helps people find budgeted rooms and hotels around the world. Founded in 2012, OYO is headquartered in Gurgaon, Haryana. The company has spread its wings of operation in thirty-five countries. OYO not only helps

people with locating hotels and rooms but also in finding homes, vacation stays, long/short term rentals, business/corporate travel needs, etc.
—StartupTalky

It literally took us five months to get an interview scheduled with Ritesh Agarwal. However, the wait was worth it—without a doubt! We travelled all the way to Indore, the city where Ishan had stayed for four years, and it felt quite nostalgic to be there. There was an event at Indore which many FIIs had travelled to attend, and Ritesh had been invited as one of the guest speakers. He asked us if we could do the interview in Indore itself as we had insisted on an in-person interview with him.

OYO is more than just a unicorn; it is a revolutionary idea that changed the entire hospitality industry in the world. Ritesh founded OYO when he was only nineteen. How a small-town boy went on to create a unicorn is a very interesting story.

'Growing up in a small city, you're mostly disconnected from the broader world.'

Ritesh was born in Bissam, Cuttack, and raised in Rayagada. Growing up in a small town has its limitations and can make connection with the broader world outside difficult. This lack of connectivity can make it difficult for individuals in these towns to stay informed and up-to-date with the latest developments and trends. It can also limit their ability to pursue their passions and interests and can result in a feeling of isolation and disconnection from the rest of the world. But Ritesh turned this limitation into several opportunities.

The upbringing that one receives has a profound impact on one's outlook and approach to life, and this is evident in Ritesh's case. His parents instilled in him a sense of optimism and encouraged him to look at the brighter side of things even in the face of adversity. This mindset has served him well and has helped him develop an inherent resilience and sense of positivity.

Ritesh has three older siblings, who are like every Asian parent's dream. They chose the traditional path, became engineers and did everything expected of them. Ritesh, on the other hand, was a kind of rule breaker and was always chasing non-traditional paths.

In the early 2000s, when he was in fifth grade, he noticed what a problem it was for people to book train tickets, going early in the morning to the booking counters and standing in long queues. Ritesh understood that it was a problem that needed to be solved.

You could book train tickets online but people did not have access to computers and the Internet as they do today. So Ritesh decided to become an IRCTC 'sub-agent' of sorts. He tied up with the local telephone and grocery shops and asked them to take ticket-booking orders from customers. He would later book their tickets online and charge a commission of between ₹50 and ₹100 per ticket.

A few years later, when he was in seventh grade, he started selling SIM cards. Private telecom players like Airtel had just started establishing their foothold in the small cities and they needed to have a strong distribution system. Ritesh teamed up with the local shops in his town to sell SIM cards by creating a system which worked on a commission basis. He also incentivized them with a free lunch if they sold more than five SIM cards in a day.

He was just a child. He did not know anything about business or about being an entrepreneur, and neither did he come from a big business family. His father owned only a small shop. But Ritesh was always looking for ways and opportunities to do something entrepreneurial, even when he didn't know about the concept.

Ritesh was thirteen when his elder sister introduced him to this very fascinating word—entrepreneurship. Excited, he immediately looked up the word in the dictionary and thought to himself, '*Kisi din ye banenge* [Some day I'll become one].'

But his mind still wavered a lot. Sometimes he wanted to become a pilot, sometimes a lawyer, and at other times he wanted to become something completely different. It was not until he was in his teens that he finally decided that entrepreneurship was the way for him. With that began his OYO journey.

Ritesh was only nineteen when he started OYO. As a college dropout he was determined to make his mark in the business world and fulfil his dreams of entrepreneurship. In 2011, he took the first step towards realizing this vision with the launch of his first start-up, Oravel.

Oravel was an online platform that enabled users to list and book budget hotel rooms. The platform aimed to address the challenges faced by budget travellers in finding affordable and quality accommodation. Ritesh had identified a gap in the market and was determined to fill it.

Later, he saw that just listing these budget hotels would not solve the problem. There was a lot of work that needed to be done. In 2013, he renamed Oravel as OYO and expanded the brand. Now, instead of just listing hotels he was creating his own brand by providing dynamic pricing and consistent experience to his customers. The rest, as they say, is history.

'When you're starting your career, embrace the tough times like luxury.'

Starting a career can be a roller-coaster ride of ups and downs, but it is important to embrace these challenges and see them as opportunities for growth and development. For a young entrepreneur, it is crucial to approach difficulties with an open mind and a willingness to learn. Ritesh believes that these tough times should be viewed as a luxury, as they provide you with a unique chance to gain valuable experience that will serve you well in the future.

As you progress in your career and start to see success it is common to look back on the early days with a sense of nostalgia. The challenges and difficulties of the past can start to seem like a distant memory that you miss, providing a valuable contrast to your current stability and success. Ritesh likes to say that these early struggles provide opportunities for growth and learning which are not as readily available in times of success.

'Evolution is the name of the game.'

The idea that a founder starts with is unlikely to be the one he ends up with. In a way, this journey is endless and evolution is the only way to success. As the founder works on his idea, he is likely to encounter new challenges, opportunities and insights that will shape the direction of his business.

Travel is an excellent way to promote this evolution and to find new ideas. By exposing yourself to new environments, people and cultures, you can broaden your perspective and gain valuable insights that you can bring back to your business.

This is why it is lucky for Indians that transportation in India is affordable, as it provides them with the opportunity to travel by bus and train and explore new places within the country. Ritesh used this opportunity to the fullest and travelled out of Delhi to visit new places very frequently.

'Customers know what their problems are; they just don't know the solutions.'

When it comes to starting a new business, there is a common view that you should build a prototype or get a co-founder as soon as you have a business idea. However, Ritesh holds a different opinion. He believes that the best way to understand an industry and develop a successful business in it is to immerse yourself in the industry you want to be in.

For example, if you are planning to start an agriculture business, Ritesh suggests that you work with the farmers whom you want to serve. By doing this you will gain a deeper understanding of the industry, the challenges that farmers face and the solutions that are needed. This will help you develop better ideas and more effective strategies for serving the industry.

Customers are the key to understanding the problems in any industry. They know the problems they face but they may not know the solutions to them. This is why it is important to constantly be in touch with your clients and to understand their needs and challenges.

If a business is not speaking to its clients, then it is distanced from the ground reality and may miss important insights that could help it improve its products or services.

To get a deeper understanding of the problems that customers face in the hospitality industry, Ritesh spent three or four months staying in guest houses in many places. During this time he identified the problems and sat with his team to solve them.

He continues to do this even today. For instance, on New Year's Eve, which is one of the biggest peak periods every year, he himself does check-ins with customers to understand whether the process they had adopted was efficient. He constantly talks to the hotel staff to understand the problem that customers face. In 2022, he was seen checking in guests at various OYO properties in Kolkata.

This hands-on approach has allowed him to gain a deeper understanding of the industry and to take OYO to new heights of success.

'Wherever you want, there is an OYO!'

OYO is a well-known brand that has a presence in many locations around the world—in more than 800 cities, if we are talking numbers. OYO is an acronym which stands for 'On Your Own'. The idea was to empower people to travel comfortably, without worrying about their stay. Being true to this philosophy, OYO now has over 1,68,000 hotels and homes under its wing (as of September 2022), including in Europe, where the company's brands include Belvilla by OYO, DanCenter and Traum by OYO. The idea stands true even today: wherever you go, there will always be an OYO nearby.

The services OYO provided distinguished it from its competitors. Since most of the accommodations on offer were run by families, the food offered by OYO hotels was often home-made. Comfortable and affordable accommodations along with home-made food became their distinguisher. That is the reason Ritesh himself always tries to stay at an OYO, even when travelling overseas.

As mentioned earlier, for a business to be successful it's important to be aware of the ground realities. That is the reason why weekly meetings and reviews of consumer metrics are done at OYO — to ensure that they are providing the best experience to their guests. This approach has been very effective in improving the overall OYO experience for the guests.

'I do not have any co-founder; I have something even more valuable than that.'

Ritesh is the sole founder of OYO and he works with his senior management who advise him on what to do and what not to do. But when OYO started, it was just him, Anuj and a few interns running it.

Anuj has been a part of OYO since its inception. He was an IIT BHU graduate, who reached out to Ritesh when he had just started OYO. Ritesh knew he could not afford someone from an IIT and told Anuj so. But Anuj had probably seen the potential of the company and agreed to join without a salary, asking for ESOPs (Employee Stock Ownership Plans) instead.

Thanks to that, Anuj is worth a few hundred crore rupees today. The risk he took with OYO was big, but so is his reward. There are many other employees whom Ritesh relies heavily on and considers them the equivalents of co-founders as they have always stood by him through tough times.

Ritesh says that there is no art to finding such people. You have to keep meeting new people until you feel that *click*. Sometimes that takes many months, or if you're lucky that might not take even a week.

Having a strong sense of gratitude and mutual respect towards each other is crucial for a team to ensure the success of a start-up. This positive dynamic ensures that everyone on the team feels valued and appreciated for the unique skills and contributions they bring to the table. In addition, having complementary skill sets can help the team work more efficiently and effectively towards their shared goals.

Employees at OYO aren't called employees, they are called OYOpreneurs. The notion is to make everyone feel that they are not just an employee but an entrepreneur in their own standing. This itself speaks volumes about the company's work culture.

Promoting open conversation and a culture of transparency is essential for building a strong and cohesive workplace. By taking the time to get to know your employees on a personal level, you can build a sense of belongingness and foster a sense of community within your organization.

When everyone feels heard and has the opportunity to speak up, it creates an environment where innovation and creativity can flourish. This can help to build what Ritesh calls an 'urban innovator mindset' and encourage employees to believe that they can make a positive difference at work and in the wider community.

By fostering a culture of openness and transparency, you can create a workplace that inspires employees to bring their best selves to work each day, resulting in a more productive and positive work environment. Ritesh says he also strongly believes in wealth creation for all team members. Around 80 per cent of OYO employees own some kind of stock in the company.

'Venture capitalists always look for the red flags.'

Venture capitalists are not going to straightaway invest in your company. They spend many days assessing your idea and looking for things that can go wrong. Ritesh's advice to young entrepreneurs is to be transparent about the shortcomings of their start-ups.

Tell your investors the good and the great, but also tell them about the bad. If they find out about the bad on their own, which they eventually will, their trust is gone. But if you tell them about your shortcomings yourself, you can build a deeper relationship with them, where you both have a similar vision for the company.

'When it comes to dilution, anything more than 20–25 per cent is too much.'

Ritesh believes that you should dilute your stake as little as possible, especially in your initial stages. Secondly, you should try to get investments from people who have built start-ups before, as they would have a better understanding of the nuances and appreciation for even your smaller victories.

If possible, you should also avoid tranche investments, where venture capitalists and other investors split their investment into parts. You should try to raise as much money as possible in one go.

'I start my day with the most complex problems.'

Ritesh likes to wake up reasonably early in the morning, around 6, and after looking at some key insights from the previous day, starts getting ready for work. He likes to start his day with the most difficult problems on his list—new, strategic challenges on how to improve OYO's conversion rates, or improve ratings, etc. He also likes to prepare for meetings beforehand to make them as productive as possible.

The afternoons are for regular reviews, business reviews, customer service meetings and other similar things. He also tries to meet some OYO hotel operators and homeowners personally to have a better understanding of their working. The evenings are for problem-solving conversations and for interacting with HR, legal, finance and other teams, to be as thorough about the current situation as possible.

Ritesh strongly believes that entrepreneurs should make free time for themselves. That is essential for their overall well-being. For this reason, he has incorporated reading as a daily habit. He also spends his free time watching history documentaries, his recent favourite being *The Men Who Built America* from the History network.

'I want OYOpreneurs to be remembered as people who impacted millions.'

Ritesh believes that OYOpreneurs are a unique breed of individuals who have chosen to venture into one of the toughest of industries. They have taken on numerous challenges and obstacles, with the drive to make a difference and leave a lasting impact, and hence inspire millions of people who will come along the way in OYO's journey.

'Chase business excellence, capital excellence will follow.'

Raising capital is just one step in the journey of building a successful business. It is important to create an ecosystem and a service that consumers want to buy. This requires strong commitment and perseverance. Even during the times when there is no capital available, it is essential to remain committed to the mission and not give up.

High perseverance is a crucial trait for entrepreneurs, as building a successful business requires persistence. If you are dedicated to your mission, it is important to stay focused and not give up, no matter what the circumstances may be.

Ritesh was one of the quickest to answer the question, 'What would you ask yourself, had you been in our shoes?' And it was: 'What is my biggest aspiration?' So, obviously, we had to know what it was.

Ritesh shared two specific aspirations, both centred on the impact OYO could make. The first was to serve at least half a billion customers through OYO, having already served 100 million. The second was to lead the creation of 100 new successful companies.

OYO's business excellence can be attributed to three aspects—affordability, predictability and availability. Every OYO hotel is comparatively more affordable than the competition. When booking an OYO accommodation, the customer can already predict the experience they are going to have because it is almost always consistent.

OYO is an idea that originated in India. Most start-ups take Western ideas and try to implement them in the Indian market in the hope that they will be successful. But OYO is an Indian concept that is being implemented by entrepreneurs elsewhere in the world, in the hope of building an OYO in their own countries.

'That's the power of a great idea, it's contagious.'

15

PolicyBazaar

Start-up Name	PolicyBazaar
Headquarters	Gurugram, Haryana, India
Sector	Fintech
Founders	Yashish Dahiya, Alok Bansal and Avaneesh Nirjar
Founded	2008
Valuation	$6.2 billion (October 2021)
Website	www.policybazaar.com

About PolicyBazaar

PolicyBazaar is India's leading aggregator and marketplace of insurance products. Established in 2008, the company initially compared the prices of insurance policies and provided insurance-related information. The company saw rapid growth and has further expanded on many horizons.

Along with being an insurance marketplace, the company further extends assistance for the cancellation/renewal of policies and settling claims now.
—StartupTalky

'I have lived in a lot of cities, and every city changed me.'

Yashish comes from an army family and, as a kid, wanted to continue the family legacy. He was born in Rohtak, but has lived in almost all the states of the country. A lot of people can relate to most parts of Yashish's childhood, but there are some aspects that few others would have experienced.

As a kid, Yashish lived in Kashmir a lot. He was a pretty extroverted kid and used to sometimes accompany soldiers on their pickets. There were times during such pickets when the Indian and Pakistani armies were just 25 metres apart. Once, when Yashish was around five or six, he accidentally crossed the border during one of these pickets and went into Pakistan.

The story is not as alarming as it might sound; it was just like going to your next-door neighbour's house. The soldiers there played with him and offered him toffee. He later returned home. This might sound hard to digest, but most of the time the soldiers on either side of the border are very friendly with each other. They know when the other side is getting special kinds of food and even share it with each other—an experience hardly any one of us can say we have had.

Alok, on the other hand, had a pretty regular childhood. While growing up he did not know what he wanted to do with his life; all he knew was that he was interested in science and maths. So, among the two career options Indian kids generally consider—engineering or medicine—he chose engineering.

Actually, Alok was more interested in the pure sciences than in engineering, and at times that made him want to drop out of his engineering course too. But those four years of engineering taught him some invaluable life lessons, such as how to live in a different environment from what you are used to, and how to stick to something no matter what.

He worked for a couple of years before going for his MBA. During his MBA itself, he started to think about the things he wanted to do. One thing he knew very well was that he would need a co-founder, as it was hard for him to do things individually, on his own. But at the back of his mind, he always knew that whatever he did—whether it was a corporate job or a start-up—his role had to be impactful. Even during his college placements he used to focus on what sort of role he was being offered rather than whether the brand he would work with was big or small.

After his MBA he joined General Electric as a manager. It was a good learning ground for him for a couple of years, but he was also looking for a role which had more direct responsibilities, which could teach him more about the bigger picture of how things work.

After a couple of years, he met Yashish and Avaneesh, which eventually led to PolicyBazaar. When you look at the top 100 people at PolicyBazaar, only a handful of them come from an insurance or finance background.

Alok believes that the technical side of the business is not that hard to learn. He wanted the right set of people to come along—people who would put the company first and take the right decisions for it; people with integrity.

He gave the team the freedom to do things their way. He believes teams surprise you with what they can deliver if you let them take ownership of what they do.

According to Alok, the genesis of PolicyBazaar lies in Ebookers, a travel company in the UK where Yashish used to work. Yashish says that Ebookers taught them that consumers buy online. He also realized that insurance was the most profitable part of the business and that travel insurance was where Ebookers were making money. It's when he went to Admiral, an insurance firm, that he learnt much more about it.

When the team launched PolicyBazaar, they wanted to apply their small learnings they had on insurance in the European context and then apply that in India. They initially started with car insurance. Yashish recalled an event in the early days when they called up a friend who had a Mercedes which could not be insured because it was the last day to get it insured and the car was still on the road, returning from Haridwar, and needed some inspections. Yashish and the team spent a huge amount of time figuring out how to go about it. But when someone was sent to pick up the cheque from the Mercedes owner, he discovered that the owner had already insured the car through someone else as they were Rs. 200 cheaper. The team did not get disheartened by this, but rather, realized that they had to make an offer that was better than what was already available.

When you have your idea in place, you need people, especially a founding team, to validate that idea. Alok says there is no single right formula when it comes to picking the founding team. When you look at the co-founders of different businesses, you will find examples where members of the co-founding team are very similar to each other but the team has clicked; and you will also find instances where the co-founding team consists of very different people but still works very well.

Alok believes that what is important is the core of what a company is trying to do. The DNA or the value system of the company should be a shared one, because that is not something a team can have a fight over. You are going to fight over hundreds of other things, but you can't have a fight about what the core of the company is all about.

Alok believes that one-upmanship does not work among co-founders; it is in collaborative efforts that co-founders tend to work better together. What role a person should have in a company depends on his or her personality. When PolicyBazaar was started, Alok was the junior-most guy among the three founders, in terms of both capital investment and experience, but the role he had at the company suited his mental make-up. And he believes that every role should fit the person taking it on.

'Skills are overrated. It is people's value systems, flexibility and ability to put the team before themselves that is usually underrated.'

When it comes to the founding team, Alok says they can have different skill sets but everyone should share the same values. Both Alok and Yashish believe that everyone in the team should be able to trust each other. After a while, what people do does not matter; it is how they behave that matters.

Many people hesitate to work with friends because they do not think they will be able to give honest feedback to them. But Yashish believes it is completely fine and that friendship should not come in the way of honest conversations. There are times when there will be conflict, or maybe times when you are not working in the best interests of the company. It is then the responsibility of the other person, as your friend and co-founder, to call you out and let you know that you're causing problems; and that should not affect your friendship. Alok says that when you are in a start-up, even if you were not friends before, friendship among co-founders or other members of the team is bound to happen. You share so many ups and downs together that it becomes inevitable.

Yashish says that in reality, we struggle when we work with people who are not our friends. With a friend, you can say everything straightaway. There are things you can say to friends but not to people whom you do not share a bond with.

Talking about the culture at PolicyBazaar, Alok says it is more of the college canteen kind. It is a bunch of friends sitting across an office table, instead of at a college canteen, and having fun. Everyone has clear roles, but that does not mean they cannot work together or have fun together.

'Customer acquisition is the true test of a start-up.'

The best part about starting something is that you become quite fearless. Even if you do not succeed, that is okay, but at least you have tried to do whatever it takes to make your venture a success.

To acquire their first set of customers, the PolicyBazaar team used to go and stand in parking lots and malls talking to people, solving their queries and basically doing whatever it takes to convert them. That approach did not really work. What eventually worked was people seeking them out through the Internet. That was what started to build some scale for PolicyBazaar.

It is also important to engage with customers. It is when you talk to them that you understand the ground reality. You get to learn so much about what can be done in the business. Some of the feedback will be contradictory, but at least it tells you what customers are looking for and what you can improve on or double down on.

When it comes to fear of failure, everyone has a story of their own to tell. Yashish claims he is a very risk-averse person even though it might not seem so. He had previously tasted one success and one failure, so failing at building Policy Bazaar was not an option for him.

'Eventually, it's about your being able to find investors who can see themselves in you.'

Yashish approached three entities, two of whom said no. One of them even said, 'Look, you're very straightforward, you will never be able to run a business very well in

India because it's a crooked place and you're just too straightforward, so it just won't work for you.'

The second investor who refused him did not want to invest in the business because Yashish did not have a record of academic excellence.

But the third investor decided to fund the start-up within the first fifteen minutes of the pitch; because he knew that Yashish was the kind of person who would never give up on anything and that losing was not an option for him.

Had he not got this investment, Yashish might not have started the business at all. He was not in a condition where he could bootstrap the business, so getting funded was really the only way forward.

When it comes to funding, investors are mostly looking for themselves in the other person. The guy who did not invest because of Yashish's academic record was himself a JEE topper, so academics was important for him. The investor who invested within fifteen minutes of the presentation was someone who had never given up in life and had built his venture ground up, so perseverance was important to him.

When it comes to valuation, Yashish says it does not really matter much to him. He believes that if you are adding value for the investors, they will find a way to give back. He says, 'If you get somebody to invest 10 million and that becomes 200 million, they should have no problem sharing 5–10 per cent more with you.'

When you look at the PolicyBazaar workforce, a lot of them have been with the outfit from the beginning. People who join them mostly never leave them. 'They may have been leaving jobs every two years while they were outside, but once they join us, they're here,' says Yashish.

Currently, they have more than 100 people who joined them right out of college or two years after college. And they are still with them after ten and twelve years, now obviously in much bigger roles. Trust, open communication and ownership are the pillars of the company culture at PolicyBazaar.

'Is it a million-dollar idea?'

Yashish believes that an idea is not the sole determiner of whether a business is going to be successful or not. Success depends a lot on the people behind the business. When he meets an aspiring entrepreneur, he focuses on the person more than on his idea. He believes that if the founder has the gravitas he will be able to build a successful business. He advises entrepreneurs to always have a team. He says, 'Things get tough when you are alone, but when you have a strong team behind you, you can go through anything.'

Alok, on the other hand, advises young entrepreneurs to be unafraid of failure. He believes when you don't have fear you will be able to figure things out.

There were a lot of similar companies when Yashish started PolicyBazaar, but what was different in their case was their people. As much as ideas are important, how they are executed matters more for a company to become successful.

'It's about people, not ideas.'

When it comes to the future of the company, Yashish says the founders have a single-point vision—profit of Rs 1,000 crore by 2026–27. 'It might be a very boring vision to have, but we are boring people,' says Yashish.

After Ebookers and before PolicyBazaar, Yashish had built a company which had failed. The problem was that a lot of things were happening at the outfit and he did not have control over any of them. Although he believes failure is never an option, he knows that you first need control over your activities. It is when you have control that you figure out how to avoid failure.

Yashish believes that the company that failed could have become something fantastic, and that was the sad part. But it is thanks to this failure that the founders knew what not to do in their next venture, and that has been a contributing factor to PolicyBazaar's success.

There have been a lot of hard times, but they did not deter Yashish. He does not allow himself to get overwhelmed by the what-ifs; instead, he focuses on the how-tos. When you keep thinking about negative possibilities, you start getting further away from positive outcomes. You should focus on how to solve the problem in front of you instead of dwelling on the problem.

'Every human being who is born has to die. Many people die multiple times, do yourself a favour and only die once.'

16

Pristyn Care

Start-up Name	Pristyn Care
Headquarters	Gurugram, Haryana, India
Sector	Healthcare
Founders	Harsimarbir Singh, Dr Garima Sawhney, Dr Vaibhav Kapoor
Founded	2018
Valuation	$1.4 billion (December 2021)
Website	www.pristyncare.com

About Pristyn Care

Pristyn Care is a Gurugram-based health-tech company that deals into minimal invasive medical and surgical interventions. The organization has a network of more than 700 partnered hospitals and 100 clinics.

—Wikipedia

Ishan is one of the most unpunctual persons we know, ha ha. Here is an interesting episode to do with that: our interview with Harsimarbir Singh was scheduled for 1 p.m. in Gurugram. The venue was a forty-five-minute drive from our hotel. Ishan typed the name, 'Pristyn Care' on Google Maps, which showed the office as being only ten minutes away. However, not so very soon he realized that it was the wrong location as it was just another office of Pristyn Care's and not the head office. We ended up reaching the venue at 1.20 p.m. The founder was kind enough to give us another time slot that same day, at 8.30 p.m. We had to reschedule our flights to the next day and had to arrange our stay at an OYO hotel (which you will get to know about later in the chapter). The lesson learnt is always to keep a buffer of at least thirty minutes for these meetings!

Harsimarbir Singh, popularly called Harsh, went to Duke University in the US but says he doesn't know how he managed to get admission to such a good University. He comes from a family full of businesspeople from a small town in Punjab, and going to the US was his first big exposure to what the world had to offer.

Growing up, he saw that every rich guy in his town owned factories, so he decided he too would own one day—an aloo paratha factory.

But life had different plans for him. After he went to the US in the 2000s, his entire life changed. The first time he saw a YouTube video was in the US. He got to meet so many people with different opinions and from different backgrounds that his stay there really did change his perspective of life.

At Duke, he got to hear the tales of many young and successful people from up close. A guy from Facebook came on to the stage in his shorts to address them, and another guy from Google spoke to them too. There were also founders of some innovative businesses coming to Duke to share their business experience with the students there, and that made him realize how many opportunities there are in this world.

He also watched interviews of Larry Page, Sergey Brin, Steve Jobs, etc., and was really inspired. He got to see the human side of business—the people running it—and realized that they were not very much different from him. This gave him the confidence that he could also do whatever he wanted to in life. So, the childhood factory dream took a backseat and he decided to get into investment banking.

He reached out to several people at Goldman Sachs but got rejected because of the preconceived notion that an investment banker should be someone who is six-foot tall, white, super-fit and handsome, and Harsh was none of those, or so he was told.

He felt very offended but took this setback as a challenge. He felt marginalized and downright angry, but decided that he had to do something about it. For Harsh, this is where his journey started.

He wanted to be an investment banker but he knew nothing about investment banking. So he started going to the library and reading issues of the *Wall Street Journal*. He would read five articles, highlight the words he could not understand, check the Internet to understand those words and read the articles again—all this so that he could educate himself about finance.

He applied to several investment banks again, but was rejected. He then met someone who was running a boutique investment banking firm in Philadelphia and told him, 'Hey, I want to do this (investment banking).' That person gave him a chance and an internship for $10 an hour. This internship helped him land a $2,00,000 job at the age of twenty-two. But during the orientation session for the job, he realized he did not really want to do investment banking. He had only wanted to prove that he could get into investment banking.

'The saga of three failed start-ups and the birth of a unicorn.'

He had two months before he had to join at work. Meanwhile, he met one of his friends and they developed a business plan. Harsh left the investment banking job even before he began it and came back to India.

He and his friend executed the idea but it did not work out, and his co-founder left to work at Google. Harsh was again left with nothing to do. Meanwhile, in Chandigarh, he met a gentleman he had encountered in the US, who too was brainstorming some business ideas. Harsh decided to join him and started living at his house and working at his office.

They realized that Subway was doing well in India, so the gentleman decided to bring a foreign food chain to India. He asked Harsh to figure out how Subway worked. Harsh started visiting Subway outlets in the country and chatting with the staff there. Through these conversations, he got to know about how much sales an outlet made, the rent that was paid for the premises, what kind of people ordered the most, etc. The desi version of data analytics worked, and he garnered some crucial information. The gentleman asked Harsh to make a prediction model.

Harsh tried to make a model but was not successful, so he went to an agriculture professor who was running some sort of data analytics for his research. He convinced the professor to help him with data analytics and create a prediction model. It took him three or four months, but he finally got a model made. But the gentleman he was trying to partner with had to go back to the US and asked Harsh to wait for two months.

Harsh did not know what to do during those two months. Lucky for him, a techie friend of his had come back to India. He liked Harsh's idea, and together they started a business called Whoopiee, which provided offers and discounts across different restaurants, in 2013.

They worked on this start-up for three years. In the first year itself, they made ₹3.5 lakh, but when two years had passed they had made only ₹5 lakh in all. After this, Harsh's co-founder left for Canada to find a job, and Harsh was once again all alone.

This took a toll on Harsh's mental health. Although his family was very supportive, he was left feeling very low. He had sacrificed a lot while working for his start-up. For seven years he had not gone to the cinema and could not buy himself even a pair of jeans. It was his parents and sister who supported him through this tough phase. While working on the start-up, he had not met his sister for four years.

But he picked himself up again and decided to look for a job. He wanted to work in a start-up, so he mailed three founders and told them about his journey. To his surprise, he got a reply from all three. One of these companies was UrbanClap.

Harsh went for the interview at UrbanClap and decided to use the tactics he had learned from reading several articles on 'how to crack a job interview'. One of them was to ask questions to the co-founders. And so he did. The interview went well and he was offered the job.

One more thing he had learned from those articles was to always negotiate on ESOPs instead of salary while joining a start-up. And so he did that too, and that proved to be one of the smartest decisions he had made in his life.

Then came the moment when he realized he had to actually join the company and begin work, and he began to develop cold feet. It was so bad that he fled to the US and stayed there for three months, couch-surfing at his relatives' and friends' homes. Three months later, he realized that he could not work in a large company. Either he would join a start-up or try to do something on his own.

He came back to India, went to the UrbanClap founders and got to know that they hadn't yet started the category they were hiring him for. He gave them a business plan and got hired as an EIR—entrepreneur in residence.

He was with UrbanClap for two years and built the biggest Salon@Home experience in the world, ground up. His success at UC gave him back his confidence and made him realize that he could actually do something. While at UC Harsh used to live in an OYO because it was economical. He did not have many friends, so on his days off he used to hang out with two of his childhood friends, both doctors at Max Hospital. There he saw the problems at the healthcare centre. And that was how his Pristyn journey started.

'Had Pristyn failed, I would have been bankrupt for the fourth time in my life.'

Both of Harsh's co-founders, Dr Garima Sawhney and Dr Vaibhav Kapoor, are also his best friends whom he has known for thirty years.

Pristyn's is not a very fancy story. Garima and Vaibhav wanted to start a clinic of their own and Harsh also wanted to do something, so he proposed that they all come together to start a venture—Harsh getting them patients and they doing the surgeries. At the same time as all this was happening, Harsh's mother fell sick and had to get a surgery done. The family faced so many problems as they went through the process of finding a doctor, getting an appointment with the doctor, waiting for the doctor, choosing the best doctor for surgery, going through the insurance process . . . basically, everything called for a lot of effort and trouble. This made Harsh realize that he wanted to solve the problems people face at every step of medical treatment in the country. He created Pristyn as the answer.

'Failure has a lot of noise, what you learn from is success.'

Harsh's success at UC taught him that you should always work with the best people. When people ask Harsh how he chose his co-founders, he simply says, 'I chose my best friends, people whom I could trust.' After the co-founders are in place you need to hire extremely smart people.

The co-founders put everything they had into building Pristyn; had they failed, Harsh would have been bankrupt for the fourth time in his life.

They had the idea and a good team, and now they needed the first set of users. Harsh believes that getting the first set of customers cannot be a problem today. Be it your WhatsApp groups or LinkedIn connections, the first customer lies in your phone.

It was not a problem even ten years back when the tech space wasn't all that advanced. Harsh recalls that when he was building one of his earlier start-ups, they had on-boarded NDPL (North Delhi Power Limited), and it is a pretty interesting story how they did that. He went to the NDPL office and asked to meet the manager. The receptionist told them he would be available the next day. They went again the next day and were told the same thing. So they went again. On the third day, the manager said to them, 'I've been seeing you two here for three days now, what's the issue?' And Harsh said, 'Sir, please give us ten minutes. We have studied in America and we're definitely going to do something.' And he listened to them.

'If you never ask, you will not get an answer.'

All they knew was where the office was, and they kept going there again and again to convince the head to sign up. That is why Harsh thinks it's never really a problem to get things done, all you have to do is to ask.

There are so many channels available today, using which you can find your first set of customers. You can use social media, run ads on Google, or best tell your relatives and friends about the services you provide, and you'll easily find your customers.

Pristyn is backed by some very prominent VCs like Sequoia, AngelList, Hummingbird, etc. '*India mein koi aisa VC nahi hai jiske darwaze pe main nahi gaya hoo* [There isn't a single VC in India whose doors I haven't knocked on],' says Harsh.

When they started Pristyn, they did not raise capital for four months. They worked fifteen hours a day, seven days a week, to build a real business which made money. In the beginning, they did not have any special app but were operating through WhatsApp.

It was in 2018 that Harsh started looking for funds. He went to the co-founders of UC and told them about the problem he was trying to solve, how he had put his all into it and had also made some money. They really liked the work he had done, and since they had also worked with him in the past they referred him to three VCs.

Within two hours Harsh got a call from Sequoia. He had only been using WhatsApp till then, but when he went for the pitch, he said his venture would use technology to scale the business. And today Pristyn probably has the best tech in the healthcare industry.

'They had everything that an investor looks for, and within six days the deal was sealed. But those six days were actually the journey of eight years.'

When it comes to building a start-up, you do not need funding or a team from day one. Harsh recalls how for the first four months there were only five people in the company, three of them being the co-founders themselves. They were working very hard in executing their ideas, and that was what the people at Sequoia saw, along with Harsh's credibility at UC.

Harsh believes that wherever you work, and no matter in what position, you should always give it your all. Because someday someone will go there for a reference to check your credibility, and people should have good things to say about you.

'Make a real business, show your intent, go all in, and build a credible network. That's how you build a business.'

If you are a young entrepreneur starting up, you should show intent. You are your first resource and have to work hard. Do not raise money on day one but make a model, test it and prove it at the zero, most non-scaled phase.

If your business is a SAAS, build software and get five people to pay you for it, and if your business is services, deliver that service without tech; if your business is a product, make it and sell it to ten people, and if your business is content, create it and get people to watch or share it—**show your intent**.

Prove your idea at scale zero and not at the one-million point; that is the genesis that investors look for.

You cannot let fear of failure stop you. Everyone has their own advantages and disadvantages. Someone's advantage could be their dad's business; someone else's advantage would be a sibling who could support them, and still another's advantage could be a scholarship that got them to college. Harsh's advantage was the fact that he could get a job any day, because he had done that in the past.

You can get a job at a call centre, make ₹30,000 a month, work for five months and put that ₹1,50,000 into your business. If you fail you can go back to the call centre job again. It is okay to fail.

One of Harsh's previous start-ups was a delivery service called DeliverOye, which he started in 2015 in Moolchand, Delhi, along with a friend. They downloaded the menus from all the nearby restaurants and uploaded them online with the caption, 'Call this number to get anything delivered.' But that did not work. So they got some pamphlets printed, the cheapest ones they could get, which said, 'Call us and we will deliver everything.' They got two t-shirts customized with DeliverOye printed on them, wore them and stood outside Moolchand metro station, distributing the pamphlets. They also went to all the nearby houses and left pamphlets at the door.

Someone called them in the evening and asked, 'Will you deliver us momos from Amar Colony?' And they said, 'why not?' They delivered the momos and charged a fee. That person referred them to one of his friends, who referred them to someone else, and so on. This continued, and within two weeks they were doing thirty-five orders a day.

And that is how you do business. Go out and prove your business; you do not need money to do it.

'Culture can only be built by the founders themselves.'

Harsh believes that people cannot change. They can acquire skills, learn and improve, but they can never change. When it comes to company culture, he says you should only work with people with the right intent. For that, you have to hire right. The culture at Pristyn is that of extreme ownership. And that is because the first 1,100 people who were hired were actually interviewed by the co-founders themselves.

There is a unique approach Harsh follows while hiring—he looks for people who are eccentric. According to Harsh, weirdness shows intent. The company also values a person's attitude a lot. Harsh has hired people who had the zeal to learn and who wanted to prove themselves, and this has worked well for him.

Once he scheduled an interview with a candidate for Sunday, 11 a.m. The candidate reached the venue at 11 a.m. sharp, but was looking very shabby. When Harsh asked him about it, he said that he had been in the Himalayas the past two days and had driven his bike all the way from there to appear for the interview. He said that since Harsh had asked him to come on a Sunday at 11 a.m., he did not have the time to freshen up but had made it to the interview on time.

Another time, Harsh met a guy who told him he had travelled to seventy cities in India and could tell him everything about those cities—their railway stations, dhabas and the best food places.

He hired both candidates.

Harsh believes that this slight weirdness in people shows their intent.

He tells us how, during the Covid-19 pandemic, their surgery business was down by 70 per cent. So they pivoted and started door-to-door delivery of sanitizers and masks instead. His team slept outside warehouses to collect the sanitizers and masks, and he along with his founders delivered them. Although this system was born out of necessity, it eventually branched out into a brand of its own and is a Rs 100-crore business today.

And, according to Harsh, it was only because of the culture and strength of their team that they were able to accomplish this so quickly and successfully.

Everyone has their flaws and no one is perfect, be it the writers of this book, the readers or a unicorn founder. But everyone keeps improving and growing. When it comes to Harsh, the one thing he needs to improve is his time management skills. He even told us that he had to postpone dinner plans with his wife because he had an interview with us. The outcome of which is Harsh's secret and isn't covered in *Unlocking Unicorn Secrets*, but is all the more reason why he needs to work on his time management skills.

The one question Harsh would have liked to ask himself, had he been in our shoes, was: 'What's the one thing that will force you to leave Pristyn?' But that's also a question he himself does not have an answer to.

Harsh's story is one of failures and learnings, followed by success. If you have a business, instead of feeling afraid about how you're going to go about it, you should simply start doing it. You will figure things out as you move forward.

'Feel the fear, and do it anyway.'

We also felt the fear of reaching twenty minutes late to the venue for our interview with him, but we turned up anyway.

17

Razorpay

Start-up Name	Razorpay
Headquarters	Bengaluru, Karnataka, India
Sector	Fintech, Financial Services
Founders	Shashank Kumar and Harshil Mathur
Founded	2014
Valuation	$7.5 billion (December 2021)
Website	www.razorpay.com

About Razorpay

Razorpay is an Online Payment Solution in India allowing businesses to accept, process, and disburse payments with its product suite. It helps the business entities gain access to all the modern payment modes like credit and debit cards, net banking, UPI, and other popular wallets in the country.

—StartupTalky

Shashank had a pretty normal childhood. He used to play video games, study a bit and score good marks—what many kids do. He was in disbelief when he cleared the IIT JEE in 2008, as he thought it was a very long shot for him. He got into IIT Roorkee. He believes that IITs are a great platform not just for learning technical skills but also for meeting people from different walks of life, learning from them and growing in the process.

He was naturally inclined towards computers and technology, so while in college, he, along with a group of friends, started a group called SDSLabs, which still breathes today. It was at IIT Roorkee where he did a lot of experimentation, developed apps and put together a lot of new stuff which his team distributed throughout the college. These experiences gave him a lot of technical grounding and taught him how to build and run something new.

There was always a lot of pressure from his parents to score well in his exams, but Shashank never did. For a lot of people, the JEE is a religion, but for Shashank, it was just an exam. You study well for it and you get through it; and if you do not it is not the end of the world.

Shashank was always interested in physics and maths, not so much in chemistry. It was his love for these subjects that made his IIT JEE preparation journey enjoyable. When he joined college there were a lot of things he was expected to be good at, which he did not enjoy much. When he left college, he decided he would only focus on what he truly enjoyed and would become good at it. 'It' was for him building applications or something else using technology and seeing people use them. He loved to see people use something that he had built! And that was what IIT taught him.

After completing college, he started a job at Microsoft in the US, where he worked as a software development engineer. That was the first time he had financial freedom, and he thoroughly enjoyed it. He even bought a Ford Mustang in the US, learnt salsa, played the piano, and did everything he loved.

Although he liked his life in the US, he realized he was doing a job that could be done by hundreds of others. He simply did not feel satisfied with his work, as he was not giving anything back to India.

He talked to many people, asking them if they would like to start something with him. Many said no, but Harshil agreed. And together they started building businesses. Initially, they were building a donation portal where white-collar employees could donate to NGOs and help causes in India. But the biggest challenge they faced pertained to the payment gateway. They applied for a payment gateway for their business but were bombarded with questions like: Are you operational? Do you have a physical presence? Are you profitable? How long have you existed as a business? Can you give a security deposit?

Shashank and Harshil were surprised as they were simply trying to put something together, experiment and build something. They felt they should not have to answer such complex questions to accept payments online.

This was back in 2012, and they were probably ahead of their time. With mobile and Internet penetration increasing over time, and a lot of online businesses popping up, they saw a requirement for a payment gateway. So they pivoted and started Razorpay.

Shashank left his job in Seattle and came back to India and went to Jaipur, where his co-founder Harshil was based. They started building a payment gateway, which in itself is a very complex process and takes a lot of time.

Initially, they decided to sell it to schools and colleges, considering the magnitude of payments that happen there in the form of fees. They went to multiple colleges to pitch their product, but the colleges threw them out as they thought they had gone there to seek admission. Another problem was that they were both very young, and people seemed to have a problem trusting young businessmen.

So they decided to go back to their roots. They were working out of co-working spaces in Jaipur, where a lot of SMEs had also based themselves. They started talking to them and found out they were really interested in their products. And that was how they got their initial set of customers.

In the midst of so many rejections, it was natural to develop a fear of failure. When Shashank left the US he made a promise to himself that he would give his venture the next two years of his time, come what may, and if it still did not work then it would be fine. And since he had already left his US job and his life behind, he, as well as

Harshil, were very committed to making the new venture work. That commitment really helped them face multiple rejections.

Shashank was happy notwithstanding these rejections because he was really enjoying the whole process. And whenever they were drowning in doubt they used to pull each other up. When Shashank felt down and out, Harshil would talk him out of it, and vice versa—which goes on to show how important it is to have the right co-founder.

Shashank believes that at the end of the day, he is a very optimistic person. He even calls himself naively optimistic, but believes it is his optimism that helps him push through a lot of things where otherwise he might have given up.

It was at IIT Roorkee that Shashank met a lot of the early employees of Razorpay. Since he had already worked with a lot of them in college, he shared a very good bond with them. He already knew that they were amazing people who could do great work. Shashank believes that no amount of interviews and filtering can help you to figure out how good the people you hire are unless you actually work with them in real-life situations. So he went to many of his friends and told them what they were doing, and many got on board too.

When you are in the fintech space you should focus on leveraging technology and building extremely good products for customers. Although there were few payment gateways when Razorpay started, payment in itself is such a dynamic and distracting space that there is always something new happening there. This makes it very easy to get sucked into the vastness of it.

The thing that worked for the Razorpay team was the fact that they did not waver from their focus. They stayed true to their vision of solving payments for businesses. They have a very high focus on execution. They are not satisfied with putting out a substandard product and are very agile and move very fast. They build products extremely fast and are usually the first ones to bring out innovative products and services in the market. All these things combined have helped differentiate them from their competitors in a very significant manner.

Shashank thinks there is no particular formula for raising funds. While some have raised money with just an idea, others have been completely bootstrapped for a long time. Neither is good or bad. The fundraising comes with a certain set of obligations and with the expectation that you should be growing really fast. So, as a founder, you need to ask yourself whether you need to raise funds or not and decide what is good for you and your business. There are businesses which work well even when bootstrapped, but if you are in a fast-growing industry and capital injection can help you grow, then by all means go for it. Shashank believes it is a conversation entrepreneurs need to have with themselves so that they can choose what works best for their business.

Shashank does not think there's a right stage to raise funds. But if you are committed to the idea of raising money, then you should keep talking to investors. While fundraising is a very point-in-time thing, the build-up for that happens way before.

Shashank wanted people to believe in the story of India and the idea of payments growth in India, and it really worked for him and his team. When it comes to raising funds, Shashank feels that having a story or a unique selling proposition (USP) is very important. Entrepreneurs need to ask themselves questions like: What is it that they want to do? What is the unique insight they have about the market? What is the unique skill set that they bring to the table? Investors are looking for proof points of their idea, their market and their team. Answering these questions will help entrepreneurs scale up and deliver on those proof points.

Talking to investors is also a process of discovery. It helps you refine your pitch, get clarity on when you want to make a pitch and decide what will be the right way to go about it.

The culture at Razorpay is that of trust and transparency. Shashank and the team have a lot of belief in growth for their people along with growth for their organization. They believe that the only way for an organization to grow is if the people in the organization are growing with it.

Shashank and Harshil aspire to create 1,000 millionaires within Razorpay. They believe that the organization will have a significant impact on the ecosystem in India, but at the same time, they want to share the organizational wealth with the people in the company as well. Shashank encourages people to do their life's best work at Razorpay, be proud of what they do and try to create the maximum impact possible.

In the initial days of Razorpay, every time Shashank thought of implementing certain rituals or policies in the organization, he would ask himself whether he, as an employee, would like them. This helped him implement many people-friendly policies and eliminate the ones that weren't good for his people.

Shashank's focus on people is very strong. As a founder he always asks himself: How can we take better care of the people in the organization? Now, caring does not mean just spending money on people; caring means you being emotionally available for the people in the company as well as enabling them to progress on the work front.

Razorpay has its roots in India and Shashank truly believes in India's growth story. He and his team are trying to figure out how they can help businesses spend less time on financial or back-office operations and how can they help smoothen the payments function for them so that they spend a lot less time in setting up, maintaining and operating their payments and finance infrastructure.

A majority of the businesses today are offline, and Shashank believes that if they are able to achieve what they are envisioning at Razorpay, more businesses will be able to go digital, leverage technology and be more competitive on the global stage. Driving efficiencies or growth on this front will make businesses much more productive, which will impact the GDP of the country positively and, hopefully, contribute to the vision of India becoming a $5 trillion economy.

If Shashank were in our shoes, the one question he would have asked himself was: 'Why don't people take a leap of faith?' He believes that despite there being so many good opportunities available out there and so many talented people who can solve them, for some reason they hesitate to take that leap. For the growth of the country, it would be crucial for them to come forward.

There are a lot of problems in the country, which will only get solved by people who have a healthy level of curiosity. Find a problem you yourself face, and figure out a solution that can help a hundred others like yourself. Let's make India a $5 trillion economy.

'Be curious, be intuitive.'

18

ShareChat

Start-up Name	ShareChat
Headquarters	Bengaluru, Karnataka, India
Sector	Social Media
Founder	Ankush Sachdeva
Founded	2015
Valuation	$5 billion (June 2022)
Website	www.sharechat.com

About ShareChat

ShareChat is an Indian social media platform owned by Bangalore-based Mohalla Tech Pvt Ltd. It was founded by Ankush Sachdeva, Bhanu Pratap Singh and Farid Ahsan, and incorporated on

8 January 2015. ShareChat app has over 350 million monthly active users across 15 Indian languages.

—Wikipedia

'Curiosity is the spark that ignites innovation and drives the engine of entrepreneurship.'

Ankush, the current CEO, recalls his childhood days when he was full of curiosity. The first thing he did after getting a PC when he was in the seventh grade was to build a website that made a lot of school information accessible to students. He did it just out of curiosity.

It is safe to say that it was a turning point in his life. Having successfully built something at such a young age was bound to leave an everlasting impact on him.

When he was in the twelfth grade, he was finding it very hard to go to school every day. He was not learning anything significant, and he felt that he would be able to study better by staying at home and preparing for his JEE exams. His parents tried to find schools that would admit him but would allow him not to attend regular classes. Out of the five or six schools they visited, only one agreed, and Ankush switched to that school immediately.

He was confident about his competence in almost every subject except computer science. He took on this subject even though his family advised him to choose physical education. But he did not. He prepared for computer science himself and ended up scoring 99 marks out of 100. After this, he was sure that he wanted to do his

engineering in computer science. He did not care which
IIT he got into, he only cared about the subject.

He got into IIT Kanpur. That was also where he met
the other two co-founders of ShareChat, Bhanu Singh and
Farid Ahsan. They were always building something, and
they built a lot of things—even a dating website that goes
live only on Valentine's Day.

**'Believe in your idea, even if others laugh at it and
doubt it, and persist in the face of rejection, for you
never know when it will be recognized and embraced
by those in power.'**

When the Delhi High Court mandated that every FIR
needs to be uploaded online, Ankush saw a very unique
opportunity. New Delhi is the capital of India, and millions
of people live there. The idea was to build a crime map of
the whole of New Delhi, based on the online FIR data.
Ankush was of the opinion that when buying property in
the city, people should also be able to find out how safe the
locality they are considering is. If your property falls in a
high-crime area, it is best to avoid buying it.

He and his friends made the map and went to meet
the police commissioner right away. Everyone laughed and
told them that the commissioner was not going to meet
them without a prior appointment. They tried to convince
the lowest-ranked officer at the commissionerate to have a
look at the map at least. He agreed and started playing with
the map, and soon found it helpful.

He sent them to meet his senior, and the chain
continued. The next evening they were all sitting with
the commissioner of Delhi Police. He did not just agree

to take the project on but also told them to not worry about the funding. He told Ankush and his team what his requirements would be, because just a map was not going to cut it.

They came back to IIT Kanpur and built a team of sixteen dedicated to this product. All sixteen would get together on the college campus and work all night. It did not take long for a professor to notice this and lodge a complaint with the dean of the college. Ankush and his two partners were called in for questioning; it was alleged that they had created a team whose members were being paid, as if they were employees of a company.

The dean sent a notice to the parents of every student who was part of the team. Ankush, Bhanu, and Farid were to be turned out of the college. But the thing was, they were not paying anyone. They had just put together a team passionate enough to care enough about the positive results of a product they were building. The dean had no grounds on which to terminate them.

But the team they had built was destroyed. No one wanted to come back and join them. The commissioner also changed in the meantime, and the new one did not want to meet Ankush and his team. They had no option but to shelve the project. The crime map was not the only project shelved. Ankush said many others were shelved too.

'ShareChat was built to serve the untapped market of Indian WhatsApp users.'

That's the thing you have to understand about being an entrepreneur. Sometimes things work, and sometimes they don't. All you have to do is to keep trying. Ankush and team did not start with ShareChat. In fact, they failed fourteen times before they could come up with the idea. At one phase of their journey they also created a chatbot offering people wallpapers, jokes, etc.; basically, one of those places where WhatsApp uncles get those floral good morning photos from. All you had to do was go on the chatbot and it would ask you what you want, and you can get wallpapers, jokes and whatever else you choose. But all of the things they created earlier were the stepping stone that led to ShareChat.

Ankush was browsing through Facebook once, spamming the link to his latest debate website in the hope that people would come and comment and the website would get some traffic. There he was seeing something very peculiar. In Facebook groups, he found people commenting their WhatsApp phone numbers and asking other completely random people to add them to WhatsApp groups.

When someone randomly adds us to a WhatsApp group we usually cringe, don't we? Not these people. They were excited when they got added to such groups. They were hungry for new content being shared by random strangers.

Ankush was suddenly seeing an untapped market where people were eager to receive content on WhatsApp—that too in their local language, as social media was mostly in English back in the 2010s. He let go of his college placements and, with Bhanu and Farid, started working on this project in Mumbai. This is how their debate website turned into the early phases of ShareChat.

They gave people an entire feed of content in the local languages and an option to share that content on WhatsApp. However, they were not getting investors to fund their venture. *'Hindi chutkule ki app mein kyu invest karoon?* [Why should we invest in a Hindi jokes app?],' the investors used to tell Ankush and his team. So they decided to grow their app entirely in an organic fashion.

They started watermarking their content on ShareChat. So, whenever someone shared something using their app, they were marketing ShareChat for free. They felt that even if one person ended up downloading their app, it would become a success. Within two years they took ShareChat to the point where investors could see it as a viable business and were willing to fund it.

That was when Ankush and his team started spending some money on marketing.

'Keep tweaking the product to get a product-market fit.'

Just because Ankush and his team had a solid idea and a potentially untapped audience did not mean they acquired it all in a day. It took a lot of time. They literally called up a lot of people to understand what they liked and what they did not about the product. What more would they like to be provided?

A lot of features were added, and a lot were removed too. That is how they reached a version of ShareChat that was actually fit for the market they wanted to serve. Once they did arrive at it, ShareChat started growing every day, and it has now became a unicorn valued at a whopping $5 billion.

Facebook was known for having killed every small social media app that tried to emerge, as they did not want any competition. That is exactly what every investor in the US told Ankush and his team when they sought double-digit funding in millions for their second round. They were denied funding, on the grounds that they would not be able to compete against Facebook.

Luckily, Xiaomi was on an investment spree in India. They saw ShareChat and got very excited. Ankush says that Chinese investors were far more aware of how to start things from ground up. China is a country where Alibaba, a direct competitor to Amazon, was born, after all. Xiaomi did not mock them by telling them they could not compete with Facebook, and they ended up getting their desired funding.

'You want people who can be a part of your madness,' says Ankush. While expanding the workforce of ShareChat, they weren't looking for IIT and IIM labels. Instead, they were looking for people who were actually confident in their vision that, yes, we will make create the social media of India, made purely in India.

'Humans have far more layers than skill sets, right?'

When looking for co-founders, it is the values that should match. The skill set is important, but it is, and always will be, secondary. It is even better if you have bonded with them even before you embarked on your start-up journey as an entrepreneur. That helps you bond on a much deeper level.

When your friends are your co-founders, it becomes very easy to have arguments and disagreements. It helps you reach a resolution together. Find someone you love to hang out with and have discussions with; someone who you can truly see sticking by you for decades to come.

'Leap over the opportunities that present themselves!'

TikTok became prominent in India too quickly. It was the fastest-growing content and social platform and a direct competitor to ShareChat in more than one way. But then something happened that turned out to be very lucky for ShareChat. TikTok got banned in India!

The entire ShareChat team saw this as an opportunity to nab a chunk of TikTok's market share, and they jumped at it. The ShareChat team took on an ambitious project to build their own short video app within the next forty-eight hours. They even beat that ambitious time and did it in thirty.

ShareChat already had short videos, and it helped them build a library of short videos in the new application, that too in fifteen different local languages. Moj, a new made-in-India short video app, was born.

They had a massive number of active users within the first week of launch—13 million! It was a collaborative effort of the entire ShareChat team that managed to pull this off. Day and night they were at it—addressing bugs, making the algorithm better so the feed became more engaging. Every animation and every transition within the app was being reworked every day.

'Your curiosity will lead you to the right ideas eventually.'

When it comes to generating new ideas, having a curious mindset can help individuals to see beyond what is immediately obvious. It encourages exploration, experimentation, and a willingness to ask questions and challenge assumptions. This can lead to the discovery of new perspectives and unexpected connections, which can in turn inspire new ideas.

That is exactly the kind of idea ShareChat was—one born out of curiosity. Ankush was curious about people behaving in a particular way on Facebook and decided to build something to tap this trend. He was not jotting down random workable ideas on a whiteboard; instead, he had an idea that began from curiosity, which he then took to the whiteboard.

When one is curious about a particular subject, one is more likely to seek out information and engage with others who share one's interests. This can help build a network of knowledgeable individuals and foster collaboration, which can in turn become a powerful tool for generating and refining new ideas.

'No school teaches you the art of storytelling!'

Being an engineer, problem-solving was a part of Ankush's education. He learnt how to build, how to make algorithms work, and how to make a product that ticks with the end user. What he was never taught was the art of storytelling.

He very emphatically insists that storytelling is a very underrated skill, even in today's world. It does not matter how great the product you have built is, but if you cannot convince a thousand people to bet on you, invest in you, or give you money out of their pockets, it won't matter.

Storytelling is not just about imparting information but also about connecting with others on an emotional level. It allows individuals to bring their ideas to life, to make them tangible and relatable, and to communicate the value and impact that they hope to achieve. This is especially important for entrepreneurs, who often need to inspire and motivate others to take action and support their ventures.

'Why was the decision of not regularly attending school so normal for me?'

Ankush went into a state of self-reflection as he started pondering about why he had been perfectly okay with sacrificing his school life. It felt natural and normal to him. If there was some other person in his shoes, would that person have been able to do the same? Most people would not have been able to.

Everyone around Ankush used to tell him that what he did was not normal and that he was very courageous to do it. But he never felt it was a courageous thing to do. For him, it was a purely logical thing to do. He knew he would be able to utilize his time to the maximum by studying from home. And he did.

Most of the time, our subconscious has already laid down a path for us. Almost everyone senses it, but very few listen to it carefully and follow the path. For Ankush, it was the decision to not attend school and study from home. For you, it might be something else. It does not matter.

What matters is that you act on what your subconscious tells you; that you let it drive you, propel you in a direction that you could not have imagined otherwise. It might sound crazy, but that is how people end up building big. They take risks. Sometimes those risks are calculated, and sometimes they are not. Sometimes they pay off, sometimes they do not. And that is fine too.

Ankush's story is a testament to the power of taking a non-traditional path and pursuing one's passions and interests. By embracing an entrepreneurial spirit and by not conforming to conventional expectations, he was able to bring innovative ideas to life and create a significant impact. In this way, he is a role model for others who may be considering a similar path.

The success of Ankush and companies like ShareChat and Moj demonstrate that India is capable of producing world-class technology and innovation. This is particularly important as India looks to assert its place as a global economic power and challenge the notion that it is a 'third-world country'.

By producing products that are well-regarded globally, India can build its reputation as a leader in technology and innovation.

This means providing access to resources and opportunities for those who want to pursue their passions and bring their ideas to life. It also means changing societal attitudes towards entrepreneurship and risk-taking so that more individuals are empowered to follow their dreams and make a difference.

When we asked Ankush what was the one question he would have asked himself, had he been in our shoes, he said that he would ask the same question of himself. And that, in our opinion, was a very smart answer.

'The courage to take risks is the difference between dreaming and achieving.'

19

Vedantu

Start-up Name	Vedantu
Headquarters	Bengaluru, Karnataka, India
Sector	Online Education and Tutoring
Founders	Vamsi Krishna, Pulkit Jain and Anand Prakash
Founded	2014
Valuation	$1 billion (November 2021)
Website	www.vedantu.com

About Vedantu

Vedantu is an Indian online tutoring and learning platform that provides live, interactive classes to students in various subjects and at various levels, including for K-12 and competitive exams such as IITJEE and NEET. The company was founded in 2014 by Vamsi Krishna, Pulkit

Jain and Anand Prakash. The Vedantu platform uses technology, such as live video, virtual whiteboards and real-time interaction to connect students with teachers in real time and from anywhere in the world. The company also offers a range of online learning resources, including video lectures, practice tests and study materials.

'I would say Lakshya was a fantabulous start. Anything and everything we know about not just entrepreneurship but, more importantly, teaching, learning, academics and education come from there.'

As they say, we keep learning something or the other all our life. Learning is the only thing that never really stops in life. Vamsi Krishna started Lakshya in 2006, eight years before Vedantu came into existence. But the learnings he had from his first venture have contributed directly to the success of Vedantu.

Vamsi, along with his three other co-founders, started Vedantu back in 2014. Since its inception, Vedantu has been on a track of rapid growth. Today it is widely regarded as a leading ed-tech player in the Indian space and even beyond.

Vamsi was born in Andhra Pradesh, but he did not stay there for long and has little to no recollection of his time there. But he fondly remembers his schooling days in cities like Gwalior, Indore and Bhilai. He eventually made his way to IIT Bombay.

'I was never geographically constrained,' he says. His father's job location changed often, which led him to develop a very diverse mindset. He got to experience different parts of India, and they all got ingrained in his mind a little. Another thing that was ingrained in his mind by his parents was that he had to do something on his own. Something big. Something impactful. This passion is what drove him to do well academically.

He never feared visiting new places, as most people often do. When he started his first venture in a very small town in Punjab, India, people often asked him if he and his co-founders were not afraid to start in a place that they did not know much about, relatively speaking. He would cleverly reply, 'It has never occurred to me,' as he was very used to moving from place to place.

Lakshya Institute was their first venture. It was the start of their entrepreneurship journey, which has never really stopped ever since. Lakshya came to be known as an educational enterprise that was started by four IITians. But they did not just want to open another coaching institute; there were already a lot of them after all.

Lakshya was conceptualized as a beacon of light illuminating the path for students towards a new era of education, where the traditional methods of imparting knowledge are replaced with innovative techniques, where learning becomes an immersive experience and teaching is tailored to the individual needs of students.

Vamsi very proudly believes that because he and his co-founders got to work with students at the ground level and they spent hardcore time on educating them, this learning elevated his knowledge of the entire education system. They did this for seven years straight. It was seven years of learning that truly transformed them into entrepreneurs.

Without the experience they had at Lakshya, Vedantu would never have become as big as it is today. Vedantu is not just known nationally but has a presence in more than thirty countries. That is not a small feat for an ed-tech company.

Vamsi fondly recalls his days at IIT Bombay. The culture is not just to do well in academics but also to move beyond the marks sheets and really explore what the world has to offer. 'I may be a civil engineer by education and profession,' he says, but adds that he never let it hold him back from other pursuits.

He faced many a cultural shock when he stepped into IIT Bombay, having come from a very ordinary school in Indore. Everything was new to him, from clubs to the society and everything else, and he really loved exploring all this. In his second year, he became a coordinating member of IIT Bombay's annual cultural festival, 'Mood Indigo', as he loved venturing into new territories.

Organizing and managing these fests for two years made him realize that he loved handling large-scale events and ventures. That eventually led him to start something of his own, where he could manage and contribute to society on a bigger and more impactful scale.

Back in 2005, when Vamsi and his team started Lakshya, start-ups were not as glamorous as they are today. They were unexplored territory, since not everyone was ready to take that risk.

'Humko sath mein kuch karna hai.'
[We want to do something. Together!]

When Vamsi told his parents that he wanted to do something with three fellow IITians, he recalls how his parents trembled at that very thought. To say that they were against their son starting something so risky would be an understatement.

As a result, Vamsi and his co-founders had to choose the 'safer' option and get jobs. But the jobs clearly were not working out. They wanted to do something big together. When you have such a passionate dream, it is hard to find satisfaction until you turn that dream into reality.

They did a lot of brainstorming, but the earlier start-up ideas they had did not work out either.

'Kuch nahi chalega toh kya hoga?'
[What will happen if nothing works?]

On the other end of the polarity, there are people who actually have viable, scalable ideas that can turn into amazing start-ups. But they feel very insecure about striking out on their own because they feel they lack a safety net and choose not to.

Vamsi and his team decided to take a different route entirely. They all quit their jobs and decided they would rely on desperation and hunger to lead them in the right direction. 'I'm really proud that we did it,' is what Vamsi says about this move. Once they got together after quitting their jobs, they played a lot of cricket and did a lot of brainstorming too.

The Romans used to burn their enemy army's ships so they couldn't retreat. That's how Vamsi sees the decision of their quitting their jobs. There's no safety net, you can't retreat. The only way forward is to battle it out in the warzone.

'You should start up for the right reasons, and not just because you want to.'

There are many people today who want to get on to the bandwagon of the start-up culture. There is nothing wrong with that, but a start-up is not the only way to go about what you wish to do. If you see a problem and you are genuinely passionate about finding a solution to it, only then can a start-up work out.

The wrong reasons, however, are too many. You might think that start-ups are trendy, a way to make some quick wealth, get some funding, etc. This is why the majority of start-ups fail. People jump in seeing all the start-up glamour from afar, and they quit after they find out about the actual struggles.

The reasons why you started your venture determine the probability of your success.

'If your heart is in the right place and you're doing it for the right reasons, everything happens.'

If you are thinking about launching a start-up, it is important that you isolate yourself and actually think about how your ideas might or might not play out. Start-ups are not for everyone, and there is nothing wrong if it is not for you.

Another popular misconception Vamsi points out is that people these days associate entrepreneurship with start-ups. 'Entrepreneurship is a mindset. Entrepreneurship can be there in anything and everything. My brother is an entrepreneur, and my driver can also be an entrepreneur,' Vamsi says, to prove his point.

Back then, in 2005, exploring their options and brainstorming ideas, it did not really occur to Vamsi and his three co-founders that education and teaching could be a path for them. They were not really teachers, and neither was teaching their plan, even remotely.

When a few kids in Barnala, Punjab found out that these four young men, currently unemployed, were actually from IIT, they asked them for help with their studies. Vamsi and his team rented a place and started teaching sixty-odd kids, helping them prepare for IITJEE. They taught these kids for about nine months, after which some of them left for Kota or Delhi for more intensive training.

The ones that did not were sure that they would not do well in the entrance exam. It was their surety of failure that made them want to give up. Vamsi and his friends motivated them to keep their studies going. As a result, eleven of them actually made it to the top five IITs.

Now Vamsi and his partners suddenly saw a really huge opportunity. They had accomplished what they had without any prior teaching experience. They could see the impact they had made and they decided to not stop there. And that was how their journey in the field of education began. From there it was a natural and organic progression towards Vedantu.

'We all tried to look at each other's weaknesses and tried to impose our strengths on them.'

Another major reason why many start-ups fail is that the co-founders cannot find a way to look past their differences. Discussion is important, argument too, but they will not do you any good if you can't find common ground among yourselves. The co-founders of Vedantu found themselves in a similar situation, so they decided to take a break.

They spent two days in the hills of Kasauli, Himachal Pradesh. During this time they tried to work through their differences and weaknesses while amplifying each other's strengths. That is the rule they have been following to date, and it is one of the main factors in their success story.

Anand believes that the foundation of any long-term relationship is built on friendship. If you do not enjoy spending your free time with your co-founders, you likely will not enjoy doing business with them either. But he also says that this might not necessarily be true for everyone.

Every start-up goes through a rough patch. Some go through it more than once. That is where it becomes important to have people who are willing to sit down and talk about a way out of the pool of negativity that results. The co-founders should never waver from their established vision and beliefs.

'Stick to the DNA!'

It is also reasonable for start-up founders to make some mistakes. The way to avoid mistakes is to stick to the DNA of your start-up, says Vamsi. He is speaking from personal experience when he says this. They tried some off-track experiments during their transition period from Lakshya to Vedantu, which did not work out very well.

The team tried some B2B products, but fortunately, after spending some time on them, they realized that they are swaying away from the core of their vision. They backtracked, immediately.

Vedantu's DNA was face-to-face interactions with students. Their education was a personal thing for the founders, not just a profession. It was what the founders were truly passionate about. Suddenly, they did not like their new plans that catered to enterprises or schools.

It is not that their B2B plan could not have been a business opportunity. It was. It would have made them additional money too. The problem was that they were not very joyful, passionate or energized about pursuing it. That is what makes all the difference in a start-up.

Another common mistake early-stage start-ups make is to rush through hiring. It is better to spend some time on finding a candidate who is actually right for the job instead of rushing through the process. Hiring someone on an urgent basis and then realizing a few months later that it's not working out will only cost you money and time.

'If you don't have product-market fit, nothing matters.'

Hiring right, creating a culture and system processes and everything else there is that makes a start-up a start-up, will not mean anything if you can't find a product-market fit. Gather the most talented people in your workforce and get as much funding as you possibly can, but if there is no market for your product, your start-up will not be able to sustain itself.

A healthy culture within a start-up is crucial for the overall success and growth of the company. A culture that aligns with the start-up's DNA, or its core values and mission, helps create a sense of unity and purpose among employees, which can lead to increased motivation, productivity and employee retention.

Additionally, a strong culture can help attract top talent as well as create a positive reputation for the company in the industry. It can also contribute to the company's overall success, by helping create a sense of community and purpose among employees, which can lead to greater innovation and collaboration. Overall, having a culture that aligns perfectly with your start-up's DNA is essential for the long-term success and growth of the company.

'Education is not going to end in our lifetime and neither are innovations.'

When asked about the culture at Vedantu, Vamsi describes the company culture as one of 'teaching and learning, with a focus on student obsession and creating an impact at scale'. He also emphasizes the importance of ownership and a founder's mindset. Ultimately, he hopes to create a culture that will continue to innovate even without him or any of the current employees at the company.

Their vision is for Vedantu to live forever, because education will live forever.

'Everyone focuses on the good examples, but it's the hardships that test your character.'

Vamsi said this while he talked about the layoffs that happened at Vedantu. They tried to handle them with as much empathy as possible. Layoffs are hard on employees, but companies sometimes have to make these hard decisions.

What differentiates Vedantu's layoffs is that the founders were always there for their employees. They even helped them find new jobs. When they say empathy is a big part of the culture at Vedantu, they really mean it.

'In a start-up, we feel that aggression is something that you need. You need to be very quick. But actually what will take your idea a long way is patience.'

Anand very strongly believes that start-ups need patience, not necessarily aggression. Patience should be treated as a skill and not just as a virtue. It takes a lot to be patient, especially when you take the risks of a start-up into account.

But if your focus keeps wavering from one experiment to another, you will not be able to give one solid idea all your energy. Be patient, be focused. Be on the path to solving the problem you have identified.

Creating clear communication at your start-up is also something that needs a lot of attention. 'A start-up or any idea is all about communicating your vision and thoughts to investors, co-founders, employees and everyone else,' Anand says.

Another thing that start-ups demand, especially from the founders, is sacrifice. Vamsi points out how he was passionate about photography but had to give it up and focus on his dream. The other two co-founders too had given up some of their hobbies and interests. If they had not, Vedantu would never have become as big as it did.

Finishing up, Anand said that the sooner you introduce kids to creative and thoughtful teachers, the sooner the child will become passionate about learning. A great teacher is literally capable of transforming your entire thinking process. You evolve under his or her tutelage.

Our final question of what would they have asked themselves if they were in our shoes, was answered by Anand. He said he would like to ask himself what made him go from a bad student at school to becoming a great teacher and co-founder of Vedantu; from a backbencher who loved to disturb the entire class to teaching classes on his own.

Anand said this drastic change in his personality happened in his first year at IIT when he saw his seniors frightened about their future and job security. 'Why are you afraid even after making it to IIT?' he used to ask them.

From that time he tried to motivate his seniors and other classmates out of this fear, and it brought drastic changes in his own mindset.

He believes that the sooner you introduce kids to creative and thoughtful teachers, the sooner the child will become passionate about learning. A great teacher is capable of transforming your entire thinking process. You evolve under his or her tutelage, and it has a massive impact on your own overall growth. That is exactly the kind of impact Vedantu wants to create on a global level.

'Anand saw a lack of good teachers in our education system, so he became one.'

20

Zerodha

Start-up Name	Zerodha
Headquarters	Bengaluru, Karnataka, India
Sector	Finance, Stock Exchange
Founders	Nithin Kamath and Nikhil Kamath
Founded	2010
Valuation	$2 billion (November 2021)
Website	www.zerodha.com

About Zerodha

Zerodha is an Indian financial services company (member of NSE, BSE, MCX) that offers brokerage-free equity investments, retail, institutional broking, currency and commodities trading. Founded in 2010, the company is headquartered in Bengaluru and has a presence in nine Indian cities. It is also an official member of NSE's consultative committee for growing business.

Zero + *Rodha* (Sanskrit for barrier) = Zerodha

How does one build a billion-dollar company, completely bootstrapped, without any advertisements, and be profitable from the very first year? Well, who better to answer the question than the man who has done it all— Nithin Kamath!

Nithin started trading in the late nineties when he was merely seventeen. Since he could not open an account in his own name, he got his mother to open one for him. His parents have always been supportive that way.

It was when one of his very first stocks went from 5 paise to 1 rupee that Nithin got really hooked to trading.

As a young trader, he was very aggressive, and in the first couple of years itself, he saved some Rs 4–5 lakh. It was at the same time the dot com burst was happening, and he ended up losing all his money in just 2 days!

He has lost all his money a few times in his life, but the 2001 episode was a big blow to him because it was not just his own money that he lost but other people's money too. To repay the debts he owed, he started doing a job at a call centre.

'The odds of winning as a trader significantly increase if you're not dependent on it for your food, bread, butter and jam.'

In his early twenties, Nithin wore several hats. He used to work at a call centre, traded online at cyber-cafes, and even did multi-level marketing on the weekends. During his four years of working at the call centre, he realized that the two emotions which stop people from being good traders are fear and greed. And when you have supplementary income, both of these emotions significantly tone down and you become better at it. So, he knew trading could never be the sole source of income in his life.

In 2005, he met someone who gave him Rs 25 lakhs to trade with, and so he left the call centre. But since he had already realized trading could not be his primary job, he also worked as a sub-broker for Reliance Money to have a steady source of income. He also started an entity called Investment Unlimited, through which he sold financial products and taught people how the stock market works.

It was during this time that his younger brother and later co-founder, Nikhil, also started trading. And Nithin soon realized that Nikhil was a better trader than he was.

They made quite good money during the 2008 market dip and realized that money brings freedom in life. Now that they had some money, they started wondering what they could do with it.

Nithin had traded with eleven different brokerage firms, and since he himself had been trading for quite some time, he knew there was a need for a better brokerage firm.

And that is what Nithin and Nikhil did with Zerodha. At its inception, Zerodha was very different from what we see today. The idea was to build a community for hardcore traders. Since NSE had launched its trading platform a couple of years before Zerodha was founded, Nithin decided to leverage the free trading account it offered and go for disruptive pricing.

Historically, brokers have been very opaque in the way they work, so Nithin also wanted to create transparency. They decided to offer just one fee for all their customers and put up the prices on their webpage. This helped him openly talk about the low brokerage Zerodha was offering through his blogs and even answer people's queries.

Another major thing that set Zerodha apart was its tech. But it didn't have an in-house tech team for the first three years of its existence. They started working on their app when Kailash Nadh joined them in 2012. Interestingly, he was able to discover Zerodha only because its office happened to be in the same vicinity where he would hang out with his friends.

But after failing to get regulatory approvals, they stopped working on the app in 2013. They had gone their separate ways, but Kailash's sheer astonishment of building software in an untouched area like the capital market brought him back to Zerodha. And also because he and Nithin had become good friends. By mid-2013, Zerodha had its very own tech team of people who decided to venture into an untapped territory. Today, that team is thirty members strong.

As their business grew, they realized there were very few active traders and that a major part of the population was not trading. The reason for that was lack of knowledge. To solve this problem, they started Zerodha Varsity, an extensive and in-depth collection of stock market and financial lessons, which boosted financial literacy. Since people were learning from Zerodha, they started relying on it for their trading requirements too.

They had always kept a very low brokerage fee. But in 2015, they started offering zero fees on all equity and direct mutual fund investments. Even for intraday trading, they were charging ₹20 or 0.03 per cent, whichever was less. This revolutionized the entire ecosystem and changed the entire game.

Another reason people hesitated from trading was the tedious process it entailed. So the Kamaths decided to provide an online platform for this. Initially, they were doing it through a third party, which created a model that could be easily copied. They knew they had to up the game and have their own unique selling proposition (USP). So they came up with their own trading website, which helped to establish them as a leader in the industry.

'Unless I can make peace with my worst-case outcome, I won't do it.'

The fear of failure very much existed, and Nithin thinks the fear is actually important, as it forces you to have better focus. If you feel no fear you can potentially be very aggressive. But you make better decisions because of fear.

Before starting something, Nithin thinks of the worst-case scenario and asks himself if he can make peace with that outcome. He says, 'If you are okay with the worst thing that could happen, you tend to be more rational. In most cases, when people face sudden problems, they panic and end up doing something very irrational, especially entrepreneurs.'

So when Nithin and Nikhil started Zerodha, the plan was that Nikhil would continue trading and Nithin would attempt to build Zerodha, and if that did not succeed within a certain number of years, he would go back to trading. So, in a sense, all potential bad outcomes were factored in.

'There's a very thin line between passion and foolishness.'

It is something that Nithin says often: When something works out, it is called passion; and when it does not, it is called foolishness. When he was young he was foolish as he was chasing money and as a result, lost a lot of it. But as he grew older, he realized that you should chase goals and that money usually follows. He goes on to add, 'The thing about quick money is that there's nothing like quick money.'

'Money is always an outcome.'

From the day they started Zerodha, the Kamaths never really had a revenue or sales target. The problem with setting money goals, Nithin believes, is that as soon as you set them you will do whatever it takes to achieve them, and in the process compromise on a lot of other things.

He also shed some insight on this through an example: If your revenue was x last year, and say, this year you want to get to x plus 30 per cent, you will have two options. You either need to add more customers or need to figure out a way to generate more revenue from your existing customers. If you start pushing customers to generate more revenue, you are most likely going to do what is not right for them. If you do what is not right for them, the product goes down and you have to start spending on marketing and advertising to get more users, and it just becomes a circle where you will not even enjoy running the business as a founder.

'Trading and business are quite similar. In both, you need to do what gives you the maximum return for your time with the best risk-to-reward ratio.'

People often ask Nithin how he built Zerodha and if they could do the same. And his answer is always a no. According to him, there is no cut-copy-paste solution, and everything works in context. If they had to start Zerodha today, he does not think any of their original methods would work.

'If you don't bet, you can't win. If you lose all your chips, you can't bet.'

One of the most important things about both trading and business is bet sizing. Nithin believes that 99 per cent of all your bets should be as minimum as possible because most of the bets are going to go wrong. This means, every time you are losing, you are losing a small amount of money. But every once in a while you will instinctively know where your odds of winning are higher, and that's when you up the bet size. When they started Zerodha, investing Rs 1 crore to start a business was a very big bet, but it felt instinctively right.

Nithin says you don't develop instincts from day one, you have to survive long enough to build them. If you talk to entrepreneurs, you will realize that the thing that really worked out was born out of instinct. And that is why bet sizing is very important, be it in trading or business.

But, as a newbie, how do you improve the process of that bet sizing? Well, you just really have to do it long enough. The reason Zerodha became a success was that Nithin started something in an industry where he already had twelve to thirteen years of experience. It was not something someone thought of in a coffee shop and immediately started building.

One of the biggest problems today, according to Nithin, is that people think they can sit in a coffee shop, come up with an idea and just go and build some product in an industry in which they have no experience. And that is the reason a lot of businesses don't succeed.

If you measure the outcome of many businesses over the last few years in terms of valuations, it seems like a lot of entrepreneurs have done well. But if you measure in terms of resilience and sustainability, there is nothing much. There are very few profitable businesses right now, and a lot of them do not even have any map to profitability.

This has happened because of a recency bias that people have. They look at the things that have happened in the recent past and believe that that is how it is always going to be. The investment boom in the last few years was an example of this. But if you see the investment winter right now, you will understand that its predecessor was an exception. Interest rates are going up, funding is becoming tight, and it will be very hard for people to raise money in the future.

According to Nithin, people need to think well before starting a business. It is important to spend some time and effort in a particular industry and understand the nuances before getting into it.

'A trading business is almost like a marriage; you have to build a long-term relationship in both of them.'

Zerodha did not face much resistance from the existing players in the market, as many of them thought it would never be able to get over the severely high credibility threshold in the industry. And by the time the bigger players started recognizing them, Zerodha had already built its own in-house app, an education platform, and very high credibility—all of which became its moat.

Zerodha was completely bootstrapped, but today it is very hard to build a bootstrapped business in India. For someone to go from an idea to an MVP, they would need three to four people and a lot of money. And for that, they would need investors.

One thing people do wrong while pitching to the investor is that they oversell and set very high expectations. They become dreamers instead of realists. Nithin has always been a realist. He always says that they are only one circular away from the halving of their revenues. They are not telling anyone that they are going to make some earth-shattering changes; no, they're just saying that they are trying to bring a better experience for people to make them manage their money better. And in the end, Nithin believes, it is all about setting the right expectations.

When you raise money from investors, they always want to go for another round of funding to mark up their investment. Nithin thinks a founder should not take on that pressure. One should only raise as much money as the business really needs, because every time you raise money you are taking on an obligation. A lot of times founders forget that money comes with liquidity preference. Every new tranche of money means the latest investor has to see returns on his investment. And the only way to avoid that is to see what the business actually needs and raise only that much. There is no one-size-fits-all, so you have to decide what works for you.

Nithin believes that you need to do as many different things in life as possible, as that will build your skill set. The one question he would have liked to ask himself, had he been in our shoes, was: what is it you are chasing right now? To which, he would have answered—'Magic!'

His rule of life is pretty simple—don't chase money, chase magic! This magic will automatically bring you miracles and money!

Acknowledgements

We would like to express our heartfelt gratitude to all those who have contributed to the creation of this book, *Unlocking Unicorn Secrets.* Their support, guidance and unwavering belief in the power of dreams have been instrumental in bringing this project to fruition.

First and foremost, we extend our deepest appreciation to the incredible founders of the twenty Indian unicorns who generously shared their valuable time and insights during the interviews. Their stories serve as a beacon of inspiration, and their humility is what impressed both of us completely.

We started this project by reaching out to the PR teams of start-ups and are really grateful that they got back and made this happen.

We're thankful to:

- Diksha Gupta, Gaurav Arora and Urvashi Singh (CarDekho Group)
- Karhan Singh (Cars24)

- Miteeksha Tailang (CoinDCX)

- Samir Vora, Aditi Awasthi and Bhagyashree Saini (Dailyhunt)

- Sowmya Shenoy (Dealshare)

- Rhythm Aggarwal (Eruditus)

- Raminder Honnatti (FirstCry)

- Karuna Damwani (Fractal)

- Mahima Misra (Good Glamm Group)

- Devyani Mishra (Groww)

- Varsha Sharma (Mamaearth)

- Nitin Thakur and Chetali Joshi (OYO)

- Apeksha Mishra (PolicyBazaar)

- Himanshu Raj and Ankita Tuli (Pristyn Care)

- Sayantika Mukherjee (Razorpay)

- Shreya Sharma (ShareChat)

- Amale Narayan (Vedantu) and

- Sagar Gudekote (Zerodha)

Special thanks to our dear friend, an established start-up founder and an author himself, Ujwal Kalra, for helping us find the right publisher for the book. Thanks to Gaurav Mandlecha, for helping us build the structure of the book and connecting us with the right people to make it happen.

A special note of gratitude goes to our editor, Manish Khurana, from Penguin, whose keen eye for detail, valuable suggestions and meticulous editing have greatly enhanced the overall quality of this manuscript.

Huge thanks to Prakriti Srivastava for editing the manuscript and making sure that sentence structure and paragraphs are appropriate. Prakriti had just the right experience and skills we were looking for.

In fact, we can't be more grateful to our dear friends, Divyansh Jain, Shayan Goonerante, Aayushi Gupta, Malhar Manek, Swayam Kedia, Prasanna Surana, Darshan Mittal and Yash Garg for being kind enough to proofread the book and give us valuable feedback about the same.

At the end, we want to thank the people who watch our content on social media and participate in our surveys. If it wasn't for you, we would never have started this ambitious project.

Most people advised us to make a YouTube playlist or a Spotify podcast instead of writing a book. However, we wanted to build something that one can keep with them for years and can act as a guide for starting their ventures.

The biggest learning we had while meeting all the founders is that EVERYTHING works out. There were successful founders who had dropped out of college and there were those with multiple degrees. There were some who raised a lot of funds while others built bootstrapped. There were some who came from IITs while others did not. There were some who were raised in villages while others were from the metros.

Lastly, we would like to express our sincere thanks to the readers of *Unlocking Unicorn Secrets*. Your enthusiasm, curiosity and thirst for knowledge are what make the pursuit of writing such a fulfilling endeavour. It is our hope that this book will inspire and empower each and every one of you to fearlessly chase your dreams, defy boundaries and create your own extraordinary paths.

It is a common belief that people who achieve great things in life, such as building a billion-dollar company, have some innate talent. The mission of this book is to bust that myth and share the stories of those who have made it.

To inspire those who are just starting out.

This is for all of you—aspiring unicorn founders of India!

If you do like this book, please share your feedback with us at ksl@kushallodha.in or ishansharma7390@gmail.com. Also, don't forget to tag us on social media if you like it.

resonates with her profound knowledge of both Celan's and Daive's poetry and the passion for language that she shares with them. The text brings these three major poets together in a highly unusual and wholly successful collaboration."

—COLE SWENSEN, author of *On Walking On*

"'We never talk about Paul Celan,' certainly not as is done in *Under the Dome*. In this gem of a poetic memoir, we are as close to breathing and metabolizing the stubborn silences of Paul Celan as it is possible to do so while honoring his life and art. 'Would you translate me?' becomes the code and kernel from which the infinity of Paul Celan's tragic genius unfolds. How else to talk, sing, or communicate with Paul Celan—who died trying to unpave the road on which the ineffable treads—if not through unraveling language? If Paul Celan's life force is genomic, or elemental, it replicates and transfers itself through us like a Spinozan miracle. Rosmarie Waldrop takes up Celan's question to Jean Daive as her own. I cannot unread her inimitable ease in these pages. This is a book that contends with time."

—FADY JOUDAH, author of *Footnotes in the Order of Disappearance*

"The republication of this arresting translation of Jean Daive's writing about his conversations and encounters with Paul Celan lets us imagine the space and time of Celan's words as they were uttered on the streets of Paris, in its cafés, under the trees, and by the river. Daive's writing is a highly punctuated recollection, a memoir, perhaps a testimony, but also surely a way of attending to the time of the writing, the conditions and coordinates of Celan's various enunciations, his linguistic humility. Yet the words sometimes break free of any context, lingering in a separate space on the page; they follow lived memory, the well-worn interruptions whose repetition finds no resolution. Daive offers small stories, but mainly fragments that follow one another in the wake of the destruction of narrative flow; the tenses change suddenly, putting into a shifting modality of writing a complex memory that refuses to leave a friend. Celan's death, what Daive calls 'really unforeseeable,' remains as an 'undercurrent' in the conversations recollected here, gathered up again, with an insistence and clarity of true mourning and acknowledgement."

—JUDITH BUTLER, author of *The Force of Nonviolence*